"church bulletin bits" #3

"church bulletin bits"

volume #3

GEORGE W. KNIGHT
COMPILER

BAKER BOOK HOUSE
Grand Rapids, Michigan 49506

Copyright 1987 by
Baker Book House Company

ISBN: 0-8010-5479-6

Fourth printing, May 1990

Printed in the United States of America

Contents

Preface

There seems to be no end to the demand for short essays, fillers, and poems for churches to publish in their bulletins and newsletters. My previous two books of such material are still in demand after several years—and churches are still asking for more. I'm delighted to respond to this need with *Church Bulletin Bits, Volume 3*.

This book serves the same practical need as the previous volumes. It puts scores of low-cost, copyright-free essays and fillers at the fingertips of church staff people responsible for compiling newsletters and worship bulletins. The selections are ideal for use as space fillers or as regular features in church publications. All the items carry positive, thought-provoking messages that are designed to challenge church members to new levels of commitment and discipleship.

Several of the subject headings that appeared in *Church Bulletin Bits #1* and *#2* are also included in this book. But all the individual essays and fillers are new material, ready for you to use as needed. When you publish one of these items, be sure to make a note of it in the "Record of Publication" section at the back of the book. Recording this information will keep you from reprinting the same essay or filler too quickly in your church publications.

My thanks to the church staff people who have taken the time to write to express their thanks for *Church Bulletin Bits*. I hope this book will serve the same practical purpose as the others in the series.

GEORGE W. KNIGHT

1
The Bible
and Its Message

---

1. THE MANY FACES OF THE BIBLE

The Bible has many faces:

It's a history book,

A mystery book,

A book of ethics,

A do-it-yourself manual,

A geography lesson,

A love story,

A passport,

An organization chart,

A self-improvement course,

A travel brochure,

A code book,

A diary,

A law journal—

And otherwise good reading.

2. THE PARABLE OF THE MIRRORS

A peddler stood in the city square and shouted, "My merchandise can change your life!" A crowd quickly gathered, and the peddler displayed a cart full of mirrors. "Preposterous!" cried the crowd. "How can mirrors change our lives?" Most of the people scoffed and walked away.

But three women stayed to take a closer look. Each finally decided to buy a mirror.

The first woman bought a small, fancy mirror. "I do not want to look at myself," she thought as she walked home. "So the mirror will have to change my life from another room." She mounted the mirror in an unused study where it was soon covered with dust and cobwebs.

As she walked home, the second woman said to herself, "I will not waste my time looking into this mirror. It will have to change my life as I carry on my daily duties." She mounted her mirror in the hallway where she glanced at it occasionally.

"If a mirror is to change my life," the third woman thought, "I must get as much out of it as I can." She mounted the mirror in her room and stared into it expectantly each morning. Soon she began to notice when her hair was out of place, so she combed it carefully. She observed blotches of old makeup on her face, so she washed them away. She saw that her dresses were torn and plain-looking, so she mended them and added lace and color.

Soon others began noticing the old woman who was using her mirror. She was invited to tea by her neighbors; she was visited by new friends; she was courted by the most eligible bachelor in town, whom she eventually married.

One day the changed woman met the other two who had bought mirrors. They were still unchanged. "We all bought life-changing mirrors," the pair said, "but our lives have not been changed like yours has. Why?"

The changed woman smiled. "It's all in how you use the mirror," she said. "The more often you see yourself the way you are, the more you are able to change."

Think of one of these mirrors as a Bible. The first woman represents the kind of person who buys a Bible just to say she has one. The second woman symbolizes the person who has a huge family Bible on the coffee table so that those who see it will think she is a religious person. But the third woman stands for the Christian who reads and studies God's Word to learn what is wrong with her life and how to change it.

3. I AM THE BIBLE

I am the Bible, God's wonderful library. I am always—and above all—the truth.

To the weary pilgrim, I am a strong staff.

To the one who sits in darkness, I am glorious light.

To those who stumble beneath heavy burdens, I am sweet rest.

To him who has lost his way, I am a safe guide.

To those who are sick in sin, I am healing strength and forgiveness.

To the discouraged, I am a glad message of hope.

To those who are distressed and tossed about by the storms of life, I am an anchor, sure and steady.

To those who search for salvation, I reveal the Savior of the world.

I am the Bible—God's holy Word.

4. INTERESTING FACTS ABOUT THE BIBLE

Number of books in the Old Testament   39

Number of books in the New Testament   27

Total number of books in the Bible   66

Number of chapters in the Old Testament   929

Number of chapters in the New Testament   260

Total number of chapters in the Bible   1,189

Shortest chapter in the Bible   Psalm 117

Shortest verse in the Bible   John 11:35

Longest verse in the Bible   Esther 8:9

5. HOW THE BIBLE DESCRIBES ITSELF

Light: "Thy word is a lamp unto my feet, and a light unto my path" (Ps. 119:105).

Fire: "Is not my word like as a fire? saith the Lord" (Jer. 23:29).

Seed: "The seed is the word of God" (Luke 8:11).

Bread: "Man doth not live by bread only, but by every word that proceedeth out of the mouth of the Lord" (Deut. 8:3).

Milk: "As newborn babes, desire the sincere milk of the word" (1 Peter 2:2).

Honey: "The law of the Lord is . . . sweeter also than honey" (Ps. 19:7–10).

Meat: "Strong meat belongeth to them that are of full age" (Heb. 5:14).

Gold: "More to be desired . . . than gold" (Ps. 19:10).

Sword: "The word of God is . . . sharper than any two-edged sword" (Heb. 4:12).

Hammer: "Is not my word . . . like a hammer that breaketh the rock in pieces?" (Jer. 23:29).

2
Christian Growth and Discipleship

---

6. HOW TO GROW AS A CHRISTIAN

Go to God in prayer daily (John 15:7).

Read God's Word regularly (Acts 17:11).

Obey God consistently (John 14:21).

Witness for Christ by your words and your life (Matt. 4:19).

Trust God for every detail of your life (1 Peter 5:7).

Holy Spirit—allow God to control and empower your life (Gal. 5:16–17).

7. A USEFUL VESSEL

It's not what we keep but what we share,
Not what we have but what we spare,
Not what we clasp but what we lose,
Not what we hide but what we use.

A vessel He will make of you,
If small or great, 'twill surely do—
Great joy and peace will always fill
The one who's yielded to His will.

—Author unknown

8. RULES FOR GROWING CHRISTIANS

Don't neglect your prayer time. It is the breath of the soul.

Don't neglect your Bible. It is your sword for conquest, your hammer for construction, your guiding light for dreary days.

Don't neglect your body. It is the capital on which you are to do business for the rest of your life.

Don't neglect your mind. It is your channel for reaching up to the very thoughts of God.

Don't neglect your laugh. The Bible teaches that "a merry heart doeth good like a medicine."

Don't neglect your reputation. It is the gold with which you will meet the demands of a complex civilization.

Don't neglect your influence. It will point other people to the living God whom you serve.

9. MAKE ME A RAIN

I am only a spark; make me a fire.
I am only a string; make me a lyre.
I am only a drop; make me a fountain.
I am only an anthill; make me a mountain.

I am only a feather; make me a wing.
I am only a serf; make me a king.
I am only a link; make me a chain.
I am only a sprinkle; make me a rain.

—Author unknown

Act instead of argue.

Build instead of brag.

Climb instead of criticize.

Dig instead of depreciate.

Encourage instead of envy.

Fight instead of faint.

Give instead of grumble.

Help instead of harm.

Invite instead of ignore.

Join instead of jeer.

Kneel instead of kick.

Love instead of lampoon.

Move instead of mold.

Nurture instead of neglect.

Obey instead of object.

Pray instead of pout.

Qualify instead of quit.

Rescue instead of ridicule.

Shout instead of shrink.

Try instead of tremble.

Undergird instead of undermine.

Vindicate instead of vilify.

Witness instead of wilt.

Xterminate instead of excuse.

Yield instead of yell.

Zip instead of zigzag.

11. SHOPPING FOR A CROSS

Jesus commanded His followers, "Take up the cross and follow me" (Mark 10:21). But too many of us want to go shopping for just the right cross rather than take up the cross of self-denial to which He referred.

Some people want a vinyl-padded cross that's not too heavy. Others look for a small, flat cross which they can put out of sight when they don't want to attract attention to the fact that they are Christians. Still others look for a jeweled cross which can make them part of the fashionable "in" crowd.

But the cross of authentic Christian discipleship is a plain, rough, wooden cross which takes a lot of effort to carry. This is the type of cross on which Jesus was crucified. And this is the cross of discipleship which we as His followers must carry. But one important difference is that Jesus Himself has promised to stand with us and help us bear the load. The same One who directed, "Take up the cross" also declared, "My yoke is easy, and my burden is light" (Matt. 11:30).

3
Christmas Messages

---

12. LOST CHRISTMAS

Somewhere, buried under tissue,
  Bent beneath the load
Of our hurried, harried giving,
  Christmas lost the road.

Christmas that was sweet and simple,
  With a song, a star,
Christmas that was hushed and holy,
  Seems so very far!

Let us stop and look for Christmas:
  Maybe, if we tried,
We could find it somewhere under
  All the gifts we tied.

Christmas waiting, wistful, weary,
  May be very near—
Christmas lost, a little lonely,
  Wishing to be here.

—Helen Frazee Bower

13. A CHRISTMAS PRAYER

Light of the world so clear and bright,
Enter our homes on Christmas night;
Re-light our souls so tenderly
That we may grow to be like Thee.

—Author unknown

14. CHRISTMAS JOY

Somehow, not only for Christmas,
But all the long year through,
The joy that you give to others
Is the joy that comes back to you.

And the more you spend in blessing
The poor and lonely and sad,
The more of your heart's possessing
Returns to make you glad.

—John Greenleaf Whittier

15. CHRIST IN CHRISTMAS

Christ, the only begotten Son of God, looked upon the
    sinful world
  and realized its need for

Help. In council with the Father it was agreed that He
    would give up
  His high and exalted place and bring to sinful men

Redemption. He would go to earth in person and through
    the miracle
  of birth would become the

Incarnation of God in human flesh. He would be born
    of a virgin
  with God as His Father, and enter into the sinful world
    as its

Savior. His holiness, His exemplary life, His sinlessness,
  His plan of redemption, His death, and His
    resurrection
  would bring to earth the great

18

Transformation needed by all mankind. So He came,
    as decided in the councils of eternity,
    and through His coming He brought the

Melody of heaven to earth. A Babe in swaddling clothes,
    divine,
    whose birth was announced by the singing of angels
    on high,
    was to bring

Assurance to all mankind that God cared enough to send
    His only begotten Son that all who believe in Him
    might have

Salvation and eternal life. Only through personal accep-
    tance of Him,
    God's great gift to man,
    can there be real Christmas in the human heart.

                    —*W. Hines Sims*

16. OUR CHRISTMAS PRAYER

God grant you peace at Christmas
And fill your heart with cheer;
God grant you health and happiness
Throughout the coming year.

God guide you with His wisdom
And keep you in His care;
This is our special wish for you—
This is our Christmas prayer.

                  —Author unknown

17. THE CHRISTMAS HEART

The Christmas heart is a gentle heart;
Malice and envy have no part.
Coldness and bitterness cannot stay
Where the spirit of Christmas holds full sway.
Joy will enter and grief depart
When Christmas candles light the heart.

                  —Author unknown

18. WHAT TO DO THIS CHRISTMAS

Mend a quarrel.

Seek out a forgotten friend.

Share some treasure.

Give a soft answer.

Encourage youth.

Keep a promise.

Find the time.

Listen.

Apologize if you were wrong.

Be gentle.

Laugh a little.

Laugh a little more.

Express your gratitude.

Welcome a stranger.

Gladden the heart of a child.

Take pleasure in the beauty and wonder of the earth.

Speak your love.

Speak it again.

19. WHAT MAKES CHRISTMAS?

The Creator made Christmas possible.

Friends make Christmas beautiful.

Music makes Christmas festive.

Giving makes Christmas joyous.

Love makes Christmas complete.

20. CHRISTMAS REMINDERS

May the Christmas presents remind you
  of God's greatest gift—His only begotten Son.

May the Christmas candles remind you
  of Him who is the light of the world.

May the Christmas tree remind you
  of another tree on which He died for you.

May the Christmas cheer remind you
  of Him who said, "Be of good cheer."

May the Christmas feast remind you
  of Him who is the bread of life.

May the Christmas snow remind you
  of the cleansing power of Christ.

May the Christmas bells remind you
  of the glorious proclamation of His birth.

May the Christmas carols remind you
  of His glad tidings which we are to proclaim
    to all mankind.

May the Christmas season remind you
  in every way of Jesus Christ your King.

21. A TABLE PRAYER FOR CHRISTMAS

*Let not our hearts be busy inns
That have no room for Thee,
But cradles of the living Christ
And His nativity.*

22. GIFTS FOR THE KING

*We all have gifts that we may bring.
We all have songs that we may sing.
We all have kind words we may say.
We all have prayers that we may pray.*

We all have love and joy to give.
And what a joy life is to live
If we just scatter everywhere
The things God's given us to share.

If you have a gift—bring it.
If you have a song—sing it.
If you have a talent—use it.
If you have love—diffuse it.

If you have gladness—share it.
If you have happiness—give it.
If you have religion—live it.
If you have a prayer—pray it.

—Author unknown

23. WHAT I LOVE ABOUT CHRISTMAS

I
love
a star,
a wreath,
a shopping
list, a crowd,
a gift, a time
of worship, a toy,
a child, a colored
ball, a party, a kiss,
a family together, the
sound of laughter, turkey
and mince pie, joy and peace,
a tree of lights, the glow of
candles, the faith of a child,
the sound of bells, an angel's song,
a world
at peace,
full of
love and
goodwill
for all
mankind.

4
Church Attendance and Support

---

24. EVERYBODY, SOMEBODY, ANYBODY, AND NOBODY

Once upon a time there were four men named Everybody, Somebody, Anybody, and Nobody. There was an important job to be done and Everybody was asked to do it. But Everybody was sure that Somebody would do it. Anybody could have done it. But Nobody did it. Somebody got angry about it, because it was Everybody's job. Everybody thought that Anybody could do it, and Nobody realized that Everybody wouldn't do it. It ended up that Everybody blamed Somebody and Nobody did the job that Anybody could have done in the first place. At last report, these four men were still arguing and the job they were supposed to do still wasn't done.

25. THE PARABLE OF THE GROWING CHURCH

Once upon a time there was a little church on a corner. People would drive by and say, "Now there's a pretty church!" At night the church would sparkle with floodlights on its steeple. People would say, "That's the way a church ought to look." The little church was so pretty someone even used it for the background in a television commercial.

One day the little church started to grow. But people said, "You can't grow. You will lose your beauty, your warmth, and your attractiveness. Little churches are so cozy, so comfortable, and so convenient."

The little church became confused and sad. Every Sunday the members talked of bigger houses and bigger salaries. Their savings accounts were growing. Their families were growing. But at the same time they said, "The church mustn't grow too big."

"Isn't it strange," the little church thought, "that people can talk about more love and more ministry, bigger budgets and even a bigger concept of God and yet become upset when I begin to expand and grow? They expect everything else they touch to grow, but they don't want me to grow. Could this be because they have forgotten to Whom I belong?"

26. HITCHHIKERS ON THE CHURCH ROLL

Highways aren't the only places where you'll find hitchhikers. Almost every church has plenty of members who are also looking for a free ride. They demand all the privileges of church membership without supporting the congregation with their money, time, and service.

Don't be a hitchhiking Christian. Get fully involved in the life and ministry of your church. Aren't you glad Jesus wasn't looking for a free ride as He faced the decision of going to the cross on your behalf? Church membership that costs you nothing is worth exactly that.

27. MARKS OF A TRUE CHURCH

The early church as described in Acts 2:42–47 was a true church for the following reasons:

1. It was a learning church. The people persisted in listening as the apostles taught.

2. It was a church of fellowship, with a great quality of togetherness. The members really cared for one another.

3. It was a praying church. The members spoke to God before they attempted to speak to other people.

4. It was a reverent church. The church's sense of respect and reverence for the Lord caused a climate of awe in the community.

5. It was a church where things happened. The people expected great things *from* God as they attempted great things *for* God.

6. It was a worshiping church. Both in the temple and from house to house the members taught about God and the good news of Jesus Christ.

7. It was a happy church. Gladness abounded. The members rejoiced in the Lord and His goodness.

8. It was a growing church. Because the early church had the marks of a true church, the Lord blessed it by adding to the membership each day other people who were being saved.

28. WHAT I COULD DO IF I REALLY WANTED TO

If I wanted to, I could help make this church the most wide-awake and working church in all the world.

If I wanted to, I could visit members who are sick or homebound and find other ways of helping them.

If I wanted to, I could attend Bible classes regularly and encourage others to do the same.

If I wanted to, I could show more devotion in worship and receive much more good from the services myself.

If I wanted to, I could profit more from the sermon by not resenting the truth when it reveals some of my weaknesses.

If I wanted to, I could tell others about Christ and His church and lead them to Him.

Of course, this all depends on what I want to do. I could be an honored servant of the greatest of all kings. I have the ability—if I really want to.

29. HOW TO BE LOYAL TO YOUR CHURCH

Our church has no greater need today than loyal members—loyalty that will express itself in:

1. Kind remarks of praise and appreciation about your church and its workers.

2. Prompt and regular attendance at all services.

3. Faithfulness to any task to which you may be assigned.

4. Glad and generous financial support "as God has prospered."

5. Willingness to support the programs adopted by your church.

6. Faithfulness to the elected officers who are responsible for these programs.

7. Consistent living that honors Christ and His teachings.

8. A tolerance and respect toward people with whom you disagree.

9. A Christlike humility in serving gladly where assigned without seeking position or prestige for the sake of self.

10. Constant prayer support for your church and its ministry of redemption in a lost world.

30. WHAT I WANT MY CHURCH TO BE

I want to belong to a church that is a lamp for pilgrims, leading them to goodness, truth, and beauty. It will be all these things to other people—if I am.

It will be friendly—if I am.

Its pews will be filled—if I help to fill them.

It will do a great work—if I work.

It will make generous gifts to many causes—if I am a generous giver.

It will bring other people into its worship and fellowship—if I invite them.

Today I dedicate myself to being all these things I want my church to be.

31. GIFTS TO GIVE YOUR CHURCH

Having accepted Jesus as my Savior and having made this known by uniting with His church, I promise to give my church the following gifts:

1. I want to give my church **affection** that it might be strengthened by the knowledge that I will serve sacrificially.

2. I want to give my church a word of **appreciation** for its ministry, recognizing my part in sending its message to the ends of the earth.

3. I want to give my church **encouragement** when temptation and hindrances make the work of Christ slow and difficult.

4. I want to give my church **faith** so it may be free to proclaim the message of peace, goodwill, and brotherhood.

5. I want to give my church **prayer** for God to bless its ministry and make its services a blessing to everyone who attends.

6. I want to give my church **reverence** as the divine institution which Christ has commissioned to continue His work in the world.

7. I want to present **tithes and offerings** to support my church's important work.

8. I want to give my **time** to serve where I am needed so my church can reach out to others in the name of Christ.

32. THE DANGERS OF DRIFTING

The Book of Hebrews declares that "we ought to give the more earnest heed to the things which we have heard, lest at any time we should let them slip" (Heb. 2:1). Another way of translating the final phrase of this verse is, "Lest we drift away."

Nothing in the world is easier than drifting. No person ever drifts upstream, only downstream. It is so easy. All you do is sit back and relax and let the boat go. You are soon lulled into a lazy stupor, not caring where you go. You may not even be aware you are drifting until it is too late and the boat is on the rocks. Satan is very wise. He seldom urges a Christian to leave the church or to give up his faith in the Lord. Instead he causes us to relax, rest on the oars, and drift along in the Christian life.

All around us are Christians who have drifted into a state of coldness and indifference. Their experience of salvation no longer crosses their minds. They have stopped caring about others who need to hear the message of God's saving grace.

Are you just drifting? Wake up now! Grab the oars and pull. Your active concern is needed as we seek to lead others to find Christ and His will for their lives.

33. HYPOCRITES IN THE CHURCH

When people say they don't come to church because of all the hypocrites there, we should nod in agreement and reply: "You are exactly right; there are hypocrites in our church. There are also hypocrites outside our church. In fact, there are only two kinds of hypocrites—those who go to church and those who don't. What kind do you want to be?"

34. DON'T WAIT FOR THE HEARSE

Don't wait for the hearse to take you to church. If you do:

You will go, no matter what the weather.

You will certainly go, regardless of the season.

It won't really matter what the minister has to say about you.

What the people sing, or how they sing it, will be of little consequence.

You can be assured of being the center of attention.

The pastor will finally know what you meant when you said, "I'll be at church as soon as I get straightened out."

35. A CHRISTIAN BUT NOT A CHURCH MEMBER?

Can a person be a Christian and not be a part of Christ's church? Yes, but it is something like being:

A student who will not attend classes.

A soldier who doesn't obey orders.

A citizen who doesn't pay his taxes.

A salesman who has no customers.

An author without readers.

A parent without a family.

A bee without a hive.

A true Christian will want to be active and involved in a local church. Give us a chance to make you feel welcome and wanted in God's house.

36. YOUR TALENTS ARE NEEDED

Shamgar had an ox goad,
David had a sling,
Dorcas had a needle,
Rahab had some string.

Mary had some ointment,
Moses had a rod,
Have you some small talent
You will dedicate to God?
—Author unknown

37. PARABLE OF THE DEAD CHURCH

A man once called a pastor to say that he wanted to join the church. But, he went on to explain that he didn't want to worship every week, study the Bible, visit the sick, witness to non-Christians, or serve as a leader or teacher.

The pastor commended him for his desire to join, but told him the church he sought was located in another section of town. The man took directions and hung up.

When he arrived at the church, the man came face-to-face with the logical result of his own apathetic attitude. There stood an abandoned church building, boarded up and ready for demolition.

38. THE DEVIL'S BEATITUDES

Blessed are they who are too tired and busy to assemble at God's house on the Lord's day, for they are my best workers.

Blessed are they who are bored with the minister's mannerisms and mistakes, for they get nothing out of the sermon to strengthen them against temptation.

Blessed are they who are easily offended, for they get angry and quit and harm the work of the church.

Blessed are they who do not give to carry on God's work and mission, for they cause the church to stumble and falter.

Blessed is he who professes to love God but hates his brother, for he will not experience the healing forgiveness of the Lord in his life.

Blessed is he who has no time to pray, for he shall be easy prey for me.

39. I BELIEVE IN THE CHURCH

I believe in the church in spite of its imperfections. The church will never be perfect in this world. It is made up of people struggling to do God's will—but people who are still human with their weaknesses and sin.

I believe in the church in spite of its limitations and handicaps. Sometimes the church is hindered by lack of vision and commitment. But in spite of all of this, the church is the only agency in the world that provides a place where people can gather to worship God.

I believe in the church because it is an agency of God's Spirit—an instrument of the eternal. It has changed through the years, and it will continue to change. It will make mistakes. But the church is still God's chosen vessel for carrying on His work of redemption in the world.

40. DISTURBING QUESTIONS FOR CHURCH MEMBERS

Which disturbs you most:

A person lost without salvation? Or a scratch on your new car?

A sermon five minutes too long? Or lunch thirty minutes late?

The need for a Sunday school teacher? Or your need for a new suit?

Missing a worship service? Or missing a day's work?

Your Bible unopened? Or your newspaper unread?

Your contributions to the church decreasing? Or your income going down?

A lazy employee? Or your laziness in God's service?

Think about it. Ask yourself these questions, and then ask God to make you concerned about the issues of life that really matter.

41. THREE GOOD REASONS TO SERVE
YOUR CHURCH

Before you say no when asked to take a job in your church, think about some reasons why you should say yes. There are at least three good reasons why every Christian ought to serve the church:

1. Your Christian life needs a service outlet. Nothing helps you to grow as a Christian like putting your faith into practice by teaching, singing, ushering, or serving on a church committee.

2. You have a testimony to share with others. The reason why you are asked to serve is that your fellow Christians have confidence in you and your ability. Your Christian testimony will be a good influence in the lives of those whom you lead and serve.

3. Your church needs you. There is no way for a church to get its work done unless members volunteer their time to teach and lead. When you accept a place of responsibility, you help your church move forward in the name of Christ.

42. ACCEPT A PLACE OF SERVICE IN YOUR CHURCH

1. Accept it with humility. You're not up to the task alone, but with God's help and favor you can do the job!

2. Accept it prayerfully. You know your weakness, problems, and limitations. God knows them, too. Seek His help. Pray for wisdom, guidance, and strength.

3. Accept it with determination. This is a job you will do well. Determine that you will do all that is expected and more. Through this task you can make a lasting contribution to the Lord's work.

4. Accept it with dedication. Knowing that you belong to God, pledge yourself to be used of Him in this important part of His work.

5. Accept it with joy. Pray this prayer of praise and thanks: "Thank you, Lord, and fellow church members, for this opportunity and your trust. I claim the blessings and satisfaction I expect from God as I do my work for Him."

43. SIX LITTLE WAYS TO MEAN MORE TO YOUR CHURCH

1. Be an On-Timer.

2. Be a Friendly Greeter.

3. Be a Cheerful Giver.

4. Be a Willing Helper.

5. Be a Hymn Singer.

6. Be an Earnest Pray-er.

44. THE APPEAL OF OLD FAITHFUL

Old Faithful is not the largest geyser in Yellowstone National Park. Other geysers have taller eruptions. Nevertheless, it is by far the most popular geyser. Its popularity is due mainly to its regularity and dependability. You can count on Old Faithful. Every sixty-five minutes, give or take a few seconds, it erupts with a stream of water and steam that lasts precisely four minutes. During the more than eighty years that people have been watching Old Faithful, it has not missed a single eruption on this schedule.

This geyser has a profound message for church members. Nothing takes the place of faithfulness and dependability when it comes to church support. Determine today that you will be a faithful and loyal supporter of your church.

45. THE CHURCH IS ALIVE AND WELL

In spite of what some people say and think about the church, no other institution has lasted as long.

No other organization has had a greater impact for good. From the church have sprung hospitals, nursing homes, universities, schools, liberation movements, concepts of human dignity, child-care agencies, and the concept of democracy.

Millions of people attend athletic events every year, but even more attend churches and synagogues. Professional sports events gross millions, but Christians give billions to their churches as freewill gifts.

With so many negative things being said about the church, we need to pause occasionally and declare that it is still alive and well. Just think, the church is the greatest institution in history, and you and I have the privilege of being a part of it!

46. THE PASSING OF SOMEONE ELSE

The church was shocked this week to learn that one of our most faithful members, Someone Else, had passed away. This death creates a vacancy that will be difficult to fill. Someone Else had been with us for many years. During all those years, he did far more than a normal person's share of the work. Whenever leadership was mentioned, this wonderful person was looked to for inspiration, as well as results.

Whenever there was a job to do—a class to teach or a meeting to attend—one name was on everyone's list: "Let Someone Else do it."

Someone Else was also among the biggest givers in the church. Whenever there was a financial need, everyone just assumed that Someone Else would make up the difference.

This beloved church member was a wonderful person, sometimes appearing superhuman, but one person can only do so much. Everybody expected too much of Some-one Else.

Now Someone Else is gone. Who will pitch in to do the things that Someone Else has always done? If you are asked to take a job in the church, we hope you won't reply, "Let Someone Else do it." Now we need you to pick up where Someone Else left off.

47. DEFINITIONS OF THE CHURCH

The church is not a refrigerator for preserving perishable piety. It is a dynamo for charging human wills with power.

The church is not a store to furnish hammocks for the lazy. It is an equipping house that offers well-fitted yokes for drawing life's loads.

The church is not a place to dodge life's difficulties. It is a place that furnishes strength and courage to meet them.

48. PRAYER OF A HALFHEARTED CHRISTIAN

I love thy church, O God,
  Her walls before me stand;
But please excuse my absence, Lord;
  This bed is simply grand.

A charge to keep I have;
  A God to glorify;
But, Lord, don't ask for cash from me;
  Thy glory comes too high.

Am I a soldier of the cross,
  A follower of the Lamb?
Yes! Though I seldom pray or pay,
  I still insist I am.

Must Jesus bear the cross alone,
  And all the world go free?
No! Others, Lord, should do their part,
  But please don't count on me.

35

Praise God from whom all blessings flow;
Praise Him all creatures here below!
O, loud my hymns of praise I bring
Because it doesn't cost to sing!

—Author unknown

5
Evangelism, Visitation, and Outreach

---

49. A DOZEN REASONS FOR HOUSE-TO-HOUSE VISITATION

1. Jesus did it.

2. So did His disciples.

3. It is the greatest need in evangelism today.

4. It wins the confidence of the Lord's people.

5. It pays dividends for all eternity.

6. It builds every part of the church.

7. It reaches people who could not be reached otherwise.

8. It brings Christians into closer touch with lost people.

9. It brings the greatest joy and rewards to the Christian.

10. It results in many conversions.

11. It will stand the testing fires at the judgment seat of Christ.

12. It carries out the Great Commission of Jesus: "Go ye into all the world and preach the gospel to every creature."

50. TEN REASONS WHY WE MUST REACH OUT TO PEOPLE

1. Unless God was mistaken in His concern, we must reach out to people.

2. Unless God's revelation of Himself in Christ was a meaningless gesture, we must reach out to people.

3. Unless Jesus blundered when He created the church, we must reach out to people.

4. Unless the disciples misunderstood what Jesus told them to do, we must reach out to people.

5. Unless no one is presently in bondage to sin, we must reach out to people.

6. Unless the penalty for sin is no longer death, we must reach out to people.

7. Unless the gospel is no longer the Good News, we must reach out to people.

8. Unless God's "whosoever will" has been withdrawn, we must reach out to people.

9. Unless the Kingdom of God has vanished from the earth, we must reach out to people.

10. Unless Christ's coming for His own has been canceled, we must reach out to people.

51. PARABLE OF THE NEW NEIGHBOR

A certain man moved into a neighborhood. By chance a neighbor came by and saw him. "I'm running behind in my schedule today," the neighbor said to himself. "And besides, the pastor probably knows about this new resident already."

In like manner another neighbor came by, and passing by on the other side, he said, "I don't believe in being fanatic about religion. I will wait until he brings up the subject of the church, and then I'll invite him to Sunday school and worship."

But a third neighbor came by and when he saw the new resident he was moved with compassion. He stopped to welcome the neighbor into the community. He showed an interest in his spiritual life and invited him to church the next Lord's day. On Sunday morning he introduced the new neighbor to the Sunday school director and said, "Take care of him and make him feel welcome. Whatever else I can do, I will do it."

Now which of these three do you think was a neighbor to him who moved into our community? Go thou and do likewise.

52. 99 IS NOT A PASSING GRADE

The shepherd who looked for his one lost sheep (Luke 15:4–6) could have said, "I have a pretty good record tonight. Only one sheep absent. That gives me a grade of 99 percent." But he didn't! Instead he left the security of the fold and went into the night to look for the one sheep that was lost.

A mother could say, "All is well tonight. Four of my children are safe at home and only one is lost in the darkness." But she wouldn't! Instead she would leave no stone unturned until her other child was safe.

A Christian can say, "I've visited and visited, but the people just won't come to my church. I think I'll stop visiting and inviting." But he won't if he remembers the example of Jesus.

Jesus' concern for each person in this world surpasses the concern of the shepherd for one lost sheep or a mother for one lost child. "God so loved the world" also means, "God so loved *each one* in the world."

39

53. CHRIST IN YOU

How can you lead to Christ your boy
Unless Christ's method you employ?
There's just one thing that you can do—
It's let that boy see Christ in you.

Have you a husband fond and true?
A wife who's blind to all but you?
If each would win the other one,
That life must speak of God's dear Son.

There is but one successful plan
By which to win a fellowman.
Have you a neighbor old or new?
Just let that one see Christ in you.

The church that hopes to win the lost
Must pay the one unchanging cost;
She must compel the world to see
In her the Christ of Calvary.

—Author unknown

54. WANTED: A PAIR OF SHOES

A pair of shoes is needed. Nothing fancy. Any kind will do. The main requirement is that they be motivated by a heart of love—love so strong that it causes feet to walk to a distant apartment or the house next door to tell the people who live there about the love of God.

Search your closet to see if you have a pair of shoes that might be willing to get involved in the ministry of telling others about Jesus Christ.

55. WHAT'S YOUR IQ?

Here is an IQ test to help you check your Invitation Quotient.

1. Have you spoken to anyone this week to let them know what Christ and His church mean to you?

2. Do you often speak to someone who has been absent from the services to express your concern for them?

3. Have you invited a newcomer to the community to come with you to church any time in the past four months?

4. Have you invited anyone who does not attend any Sunday school or church to come with you?

5. Have you taken time to greet the people who sit next to you in the pew before or after the church services?

6. Do you pray that the Holy Spirit will burden you for lost people around you?

There are people around you who are waiting for someone to invite them to church. Increase your IQ this week. Invite someone to worship and study God's Word with you at your church.

56. TAKE THE TIME TO ASK

A well-known businessman bought a large insurance policy on himself. It was so large that the newspapers published the story. One of the man's friends, an insurance agent, asked why he didn't buy the policy from him. The businessman replied, "You never asked me."

Could it be that some of our neighbors would attend Sunday school next Sunday if we just asked them? Could it be that someone will never accept Christ because we never asked them? People are just waiting to be asked. Make sure you take the time to ask.

57. PRESCRIPTION FOR REVIVAL

If all the sleeping folk will wake up,
If all the lukewarm folk will fire up,
If all the dishonest folk will confess up,
If all the disgruntled folk will cheer up,
If all the estranged folk will make up,
If all the gossipers will shut up,
If all the true soldiers will stand up,
If all the dry bones will shake up,
If all the church members will pray up . . .
Then we can have a revival!

—R. G. Lee

58. EVIDENCE OF REVIVAL

How can we tell whether our church has been revived? One obvious clue is renewed enthusiasm about our faith and our church. This enthusiasm must be translated into actions. Some of these actions include:

1. An eagerness to worship God with fellow Christians every Lord's day.

2. A burning desire to visit and share our faith with those who need to know Christ.

3. A desire to study God's Word in private as well as at Sunday school.

4. A spirit of prayer for God's will to be done in our lives and in the life of our church.

5. A willingness to share our material blessings to support the work of our church at home and around the world.

59. GOD'S PEOPLE ARE THE KEY TO REVIVAL

If God's people will:

Recognize their need,

Confess their sins,

Turn from their wicked ways,

Pray for their lost friends,

Claim the promises of the Bible,

Go out to win others in His name,

Bring their friends to God's house,

Pray for the revival speaker,

Show their Christian joy by how they live,

And give first place to the Lord in their lives,

Then we can have a revival!

60. GUIDELINES FOR VISITATION

Value the life of every person.
isualize the tragic condition of the lost.
erify the name, address, and spiritual need of the prospect.

Invest time in prayer for the person before visiting.
nvolve another Christian in visiting the prospect with you.
nvite the person to Sunday school and worship services.

Seek to help the person know the Lord.
trive to understand the person's real condition.
tay long enough to accomplish the purpose of your visit.

Introduce yourself in a friendly manner.
nform the person of the purpose of your visit.
dentify other members of the family who need Christ.

Tell about your own conversion experience.
ry to lead the person to a decision for Christ.
rust the Lord for the results.

6
Father's Day Messages

61. A FATHER'S DAY PRAYER

Lord, thank you for fathers and their special place in the life of the family. Grant that the fathers of our church and our nation shall learn and accept the unique role you have given to them. Give them the spiritual discernment to lead their children to know God as Father through faith in Thee. We pray that fathers will have the wisdom to express your truth in such a way that their home will be a heaven on earth because you are in it. Through Jesus Christ our Lord. Amen.

62. A FATHER'S ADVICE

The best advice I ever had
Was given to me by my dad;
These occasions being rare,
I listened with the greatest care.

My dad began by telling me
About his life, that I might see

The things he did, both bad and good,
While wondering if I understood.

"Let heart and conscience be your guide;
Be not possessed with foolish pride.
Do the things that you must do,
Ignore what others think of you.

Nor be ashamed of your ideas,
But live them and expel your fears.
Your life is yours and yours alone—
A treasure God has made your own.

If you are wrong but think you're right,
Instinct calls to stand and fight,
But better to surrender pride
And try to see the other side."

These were the words my father told
And I have treasured them as gold;
And Somewhere, in a Far-Off land,
My father knows I understand.

—Ernest Smith

63. PORTRAIT OF A FATHER

A father's voice is good for calling kids home for supper, reading the part of Papa Bear, laying down the law, fussing about the budget, and for saying, "I love you" to Mother.

A father's arms are good for throwing footballs, baiting fishhooks, repairing vacuum cleaners, swatting the dog with a newspaper, waxing the car, helping a neighbor, opening ketchup jars, moving the furniture, and hugging his children.

Fathers drive cars, trucks, airplanes, lawnmowers, bowling balls, golf clubs—and their wives crazy by watching sports on TV.

A father likes to growl sometimes about inflation, missing buttons, cereal on his chair, bicycles in the driveway, the town council, fancy casseroles, the empty gas tank, and candlelight dinners. But his growl is usually worse than his bite.

A father likes steak, roast beef, anything that goes "va-room," wrestling with his son, the end of violin lessons, wilderness vacations, and the dress that Mother wore on her honeymoon.

The best time for Father is when, returning home from an outing, some member of the family says, "That was a super day, Dad. Thanks for taking us."

Being a father is a wonderful experience. Being a good father is an even greater joy. But being a Christian father who honors God by the way he cares for his family is the greatest joy of all.

64. IN PRAISE OF FATHERS

Fathers are wonderful people,
Too little understood,
And we do not sing their praises
As often as we should.

Somehow Father seems to be
The man who pays the bills,
While Mother binds up little hurts
And nurses all our ills.

Father struggles every day
To live up to his image
As protector and provider
And "hero of the scrimmage."

And perhaps that is the reason
We sometimes get the notion
That fathers are not subject
To the thing we call emotion.

But if you look inside Dad's heart
Where no one else can see,
You'll find he's sentimental
And as soft as he can be.

And like our Heavenly Father,
He's a guardian and a guide—
Someone whom you can count on
To walk close by your side.

—Author unknown

65. A GODLY FATHER

God had something special in mind when He made the first father. He assigned him a specific role in life. All of a father's activities are measured against that standard.

A little boy needs a father. He needs someone to teach him how to be a man, to take him by the hand and lead him through the maze of life, to teach him to be strong, gentle, loving, and to be a defender of the right.

A little girl needs a father, too. She needs a father to protect her, to counsel her on life's problems, to teach her how to be a woman.

The home needs a father to serve as provider, protector, spiritual leader, and counselor. While the world seldom hears what a father says to his children, the effects of his counsel will be felt by the next generation, and the next, and the next.

The Bible has these words of instruction for fathers: "Husbands, love your wives, even as Christ also loved the church" (Eph. 5:25). "Fathers, provoke not your children to wrath: but bring them up in the nurture and admonition of the Lord" (Eph. 6:4).

7
Home and Family Life

66. WHERE LOVE ABIDES

I turned an ancient poet's book
And found upon the page,
"Stone walls do not a prison make
Or iron bars a cage."

Yes, that is true, and something more,
You'll find where'er you roam
That marble floors and gilded walls
Can never make a home.

But everywhere that love abides,
And friendship is a guest
Is surely home, and home sweet home,
For there the soul can rest.

—Henry Van Dyke

67. THE STORY OF A BOY

Once there was a little boy. When he was six weeks old his
parents turned him over to a babysitter while they worked

and partied. When he was three, everybody said "How cute" as he sang a beer commercial jingle he had heard on television. When he was six, his father occasionally dropped him off for Sunday school on his way to the golf course.

When he was eight, he learned to play cards by watching his parents. When he was ten, he spent his after-school hours reading comic books and playing video games with his friends at a nearby convenience store.

When he was thirteen, he told his parents that other boys his age didn't have to go to Sunday school or church, so they agreed that he could do as he wished. When he was sixteen, the police phoned his parents one night. "We have your son," they said. "He's in trouble."

"I don't believe it," his father replied. "It can't be *my* son!"

68. TEN QUESTIONS TO ASK ABOUT YOUR HOME

1. Is my mate closer to God or more distant from Him because of me?

2. Can my family see that doing God's will is the most important priority in my life?

3. Does our family take a few minutes each day to read and discuss God's Word?

4. Do all the family members pray together at least once a day in addition to mealtimes?

5. Is our family ministering to others who are needy, lonely, and struggling, or are we self-sufficient and isolated from those whom Christ came to serve?

6. Does our family talk to one another in loving tones as though we appreciate and value each other?

7. Does our family set aside time for enjoyable recreational activities together?

8. Does each member of the family know that he is valued and loved? Has this been openly and affectionately expressed to him?

49

9. Are our children growing up to have self-esteem and confidence in who they are? Can each child look at himself in the mirror and say, "I'm glad I'm me"?

10. If I had it to do all over again, would I marry the same person, have the same children, and give myself the same life?

69. A DEDICATION PRAYER FOR PARENTS

O God, we thank thee that thou has given us this child. Help us to be fit for this great privilege and responsibility which has come to us. Help us to teach him and to train him as we ought. Help us to bring him to thee, not only by our words but also by our example. Help us to give him a home that he will always remember with gratitude and joy. Help us so to live that some day he will thank God for every time he remembers his parents. Help us so to bring him up that at the last it shall be seen that we have not failed in the trust which thou hast placed in us. Through Jesus Christ our Lord. Amen.

—*William Barclay*

70. FIVE VALENTINES TO GIVE YOUR CHILDREN

1. **Acceptance.** Teach them they are loved for who they are. Give this gift with a kiss.

2. **Self-confidence.** Help them understand that they can trust themselves. Give this gift with a hug.

3. **Life without needless fears.** Don't let them see you as a worrier. Give this gift with laughter.

4. **Appreciation.** Help them become people with a spark who enjoy all of life and everything around them. Give this gift as they go out the door.

5. **Faith.** Introduce them to God, the best friend they will ever have. Give this gift by taking them to Sunday school and worship services every Lord's day.

71. BEATITUDES FOR MARRIED COUPLES

Blessed are the husband and wife who continue to be affectionate, considerate, and loving through all the days of their life together.

Blessed are the husband and wife who are as polite and courteous to one another as they are to their friends.

Blessed are the husband and wife who have a sense of humor, for this will be a handy shock absorber.

Blessed are they who love each other more than any other person in the world, and who joyfully fulfill their marriage vow of a lifetime of fidelity as husband and wife.

Blessed are they who thank God for their blessings, and who set aside some time each day for the reading of the Bible and prayer.

Blessed are they who never speak harshly to each other and who make their home a place of mutual encouragement and love.

Blessed are the husband and wife who can work out their problems without interference from relatives.

Blessed are the husband and wife who dedicate their lives and their home to the advancement of Christ and His kingdom.

72. THE PLASTIC YEARS

They pass so quickly, the days of youth,
And the children change so fast,
And soon they harden in the mold,
And the plastic years are past.

Then shape their lives while they are young,
This be our prayer, our aim,
That every child we meet shall bear
The imprint of His name.

—Author unknown

73. A PRAYER FOR THOSE WHO LIVE ALONE

I live alone, dear Lord,
Stay by my side,
In all my daily needs
Be thou my guide.

Grant me good health,
For that indeed, I pray,
To carry on my work
From day to day.

Keep pure my mind,
My thoughts, my every deed;
Let me be kind, unselfish,
In my neighbor's needs.

Spare me from fire, from flood,
Malicious tongues,
From thieves, from fear,
And evil ones.

If sickness or an accident befall,
Then humbly, Lord, I pray,
Hear thou my call,
And when I'm feeling low or in despair,
Lift up my heart
And help me in my prayer.

I live alone, dear Lord,
Yet have no fear,
Because I feel your presence,
Ever near.

—Author unknown

74. YOUR HOME IS BUGGED!

Yes, your home is bugged. In every home there are two microphones per child—one in each ear. These highly sensitive instruments pick up the table prayers, the hymns sung, ordinary conversations, incidental remarks, and a variety of words. These all-absorbing microphones transmit all they hear to highly impressionable minds. Be careful what you say.

75. BEATITUDES FOR FRIENDS OF THE AGING

Blessed are they who understand
My faltering step and shaking hand.
Blessed are they who seem to know
That my eyes are dim and my wits are slow.

Blessed are they who looked away
When my coffee spilled at the table today.
Blessed are they with a cheery smile.
Who stop to chat for a little while.

Blessed are they who never say,
"You've told that story twice today."
Blessed are they who know the ways
To bring back memories of yesterdays.

Blessed are they who ease the days
On my journey home in loving ways.

—Esther Mary Walker

76. ADVICE TO PARENTS FROM CHILDREN

1. Don't spoil me. I know quite well that I should not have all that I ask for. I'm testing you.

2. Don't be afraid to be firm with me. I prefer it; it makes me feel more secure.

3. Don't let me form bad habits. I have to rely on you to detect them early in my growing-up years.

4. Don't make me feel smaller than I am. It only makes me behave as if I'm older and more mature.

5. Don't correct me in front of people if you can help it. I'll pay greater attention if you talk quietly with me in private.

6. Don't make me feel that my mistakes are sins. It upsets my sense of values.

7. Don't protect me from consequences. I need to learn the painful way sometimes.

8. Don't get upset when I say, "I hate you." It isn't you I hate but your power over me.

9. Don't nag. If you do, I will have to protect myself by pretending to be deaf.

10. Don't take too much notice of my small ailments. Sometimes this is just my way of begging for attention.

77. OUR WEDDING ANNIVERSARY

This is the anniversary of the day of days
   For us, when we with faith and hope
Fared forth together; solemn and yet gay
   We faced the future, for life's upward slope.

It was joyous going, and we never thought
   That there might be worries—hours of pain
And sleepless nights that left one overwrought—
   That loss would often come instead of gain.

But looking back, the time has not seemed long,
   Although the road, for us, was sometimes rough . . .
We have grown quiet and the buoyant song
   Once in our hearts sings low, and yet enough
Of loveliness still lives to make amend
To us, for all the ills life chose to send.

—Margaret E. Bruner

78. WANTED: PARENTS WHO WILL INFLUENCE THEIR CHILDREN

Some parents say, "We will not influence our children in making choices and decisions in matters of religion." Why not?

We can rest assured that the ads in all the media will try to influence our children. So will the movies, the neighbors, and their friends. We use our influence over flowers, vegetables, friends. Shall we ignore our own children? May God forgive us if we do.

There's really no such thing as a perfect family. But if there were, it would include family members like the following Bible personalities:

Fathers like Abraham. "He will command his children and his household after him, and they shall keep the way of the Lord" (Gen. 18:19).

Mothers like Hannah. Hannah declared that "as long as he [her son] liveth, he shall be lent to the Lord" (1 Sam. 1:28).

Boys like Jesus. He returned with His parents to Nazareth "and was subject unto them" (Luke 2:51).

Girls like the one who told her mistress that God would heal Naaman's leprosy (2 Kings 5:3).

Brothers like Nehemiah and Hanani, who served God together (Neh. 7:2).

Sisters like Mary and Martha, who received Jesus into their home and into their hearts (Luke 10:38–39).

8
Humor

80. WHAT THOSE WORDS REALLY MEAN

Christians don't always say what they mean. The following statements are often heard around the church. Notice the true translation of each pious phrase.

1. "It needs to be done" means, "I'm not going to do anything about it, but the church ought to."

2. "I've heard some criticism" means, "I'm against it, but I don't want to stand by myself."

3. "The whole church is upset" usually means, "Two or three loudmouths have said something against it."

4. "It might bring criticism" means, "I know it should be done, but it takes too much effort for me to get involved."

5. "If memory serves me right" really means, "I'm going to say something that I'm not sure is true or false, but if somebody discovers I'm wrong, then I can always blame my memory."

6. "I'll be there if I'm not providentially hindered" means, "If I'm not there, you can blame it on God."

7. "I'll come every time I can" means, "If I don't have something better to do, I'll be there."

8. "I won't promise but I'll do my best" means, "Don't expect much out of me."

81. WHO REALLY BROKE DOWN THE WALLS OF JERICHO?

The pastor visited a class of boys one Sunday morning to find out what they were learning during Bible study. "Who broke down the walls of Jericho?" he asked.

"Not me, sir," each boy replied.

"Is this typical of your class?" the pastor asked the teacher.

"These are honest boys and I believe them," the teacher replied. "I don't believe they would do a thing like that."

Frustrated and discouraged, the pastor told the Sunday school director about his visit to the class and the response of the boys and their teacher.

"Pastor, I have known that teacher and those boys for a long time," the director replied. "If they said they didn't do it, that's good enough for me."

Next, the minister brought the matter before the official board of the church. They discussed it for two hours, then reported: "Pastor, we see no need to get upset about a little thing like this. Let's just pay for any damages involved, and charge it to general church maintenance."

82. LAMENT OF THE LENDER

I think that I shall never see
The dollar that I loaned to thee—
A dollar that I could have spent
For varied forms of merriment.

The one I loaned to you so gladly,
The same one I now need so badly;
For whose return I had great hope,
Just like an optimistic dope.

But dollars loaned to folks like thee
Are not returned to fools like me.

—Author unknown

83. NEEDED: MORE POCKET-WATCH CHRISTIANS

Many Christians are like wheelbarrows: not good unless pushed.

Others are like canoes: they need to be paddled.

Some are like kites: if you don't keep a string on them, they fly away.

Still others are like balloons: full of wind and just waiting for a chance to explode.

Then there are others like footballs: you can't tell which way they will bounce.

But, praise the Lord, many Christians are like good pocket watches: with open faces and busy hands, they are well-regulated and full of good works. Christians like these are the backbone of the church.

84. WHY ARE FIRE TRUCKS RED?

Fire trucks have four wheels and eight fire fighters; four plus eight equals twelve. There are twelve inches in a foot. A foot is a ruler. Queen Elizabeth is a ruler, and the *Queen Elizabeth* is one of the largest ships on the seven seas. Seas have fish. Fish have fins. The Finns fought the Russians. The Russians are red. Fire trucks are always rushin'. Therefore, fire trucks are usually red!

If you think *this* is wild, you ought to hear some people trying to explain why they do not attend Sunday school and church on Sunday morning!

9
Independence Day, Freedom, and Patriotism

---

85. OUR COUNTRY WE COMMEND

Lord, while for all mankind we pray,
Of every clime and coast,
O hear us for our native land—
The land we love the most.

Unite us in the sacred love
Of knowledge, truth, and Thee;
And let our hills and valleys shout
The songs of liberty.

Lord of the nations, thus to Thee
Our country we commend;
Be thou her refuge and her trust,
Her everlasting friend.

—Author unknown

86. A PRAYER FOR OUR COUNTRY

Lord God of heaven, who hath so lavishly blessed this land, make us, thy people, to be humble. Keep us ever aware that the good things we enjoy have come from thee, that thou didst lend them to us.

Impress upon our smugness the knowledge that we are not owners, but stewards. Remind us, lest we become filled with conceit, that one day a reckoning will be required of us.

Sanctify our love of country, that our boasting may be turned into humility and our pride into a ministry to people everywhere. Help us to make this God's own country, by living like God's own people. Amen.

—Peter Marshall

87. FORMULA FOR A STRONG NATION

I know three things must always be
To keep a nation strong and free.
One is a hearthstone bright and dear,
With busy, happy loved ones near.

One is a ready heart and hand
To love, and serve, and keep the land.
One is a worn and beaten way
To where the people go to pray.

So long as these are kept alive,
Nation and people will survive.
God, keep them always, everywhere—
The home, the heart, the place of prayer.

—Author unknown

88. GOD BLESS OUR LAND

Maker of earth and sea,
What shall we render thee?
All things are thine!
Ours but from day to day
Still with one heart to pray,
"God bless our land always,
This land of thine."

Mighty in brotherhood,
Mighty for God and Good,
  Let us be thine.
Here let the nations see
Toil from the curse set free,
Labor and liberty,
  Our cause—and thine.

Strong to defend the right,
Proud in all nations' sight,
  Lowly in thine.
One in all noble fame,
Still be our path the same,
Onward in freedom's name,
  Upward in thine.

—Author unknown

89. THE FLAG

O banner blazoned in the sky,
  Fling out your royal red;
Each deeper hue to crimson dye
  Won by our sainted dead.

Ye bands of snowy whiteness clean
  That bar the waning day,
Stand as the prophecy of things unseen
  Toward which we hew our way.

Fair field of blue, a symbol true
  Of Right, of Faith, of God,
O'erarch us as we seek anew
  The paths our fathers trod.

Ye clustered stars that gleam above,
  Our darkness turn to light;
Reveal to men heaven's law of love—
  Then ends the world's long night.

—Henry C. Potter

90. A MONUMENT OF PEACE AND LIBERTY

Let our object be our country, our whole country, and nothing but our country. And, by the blessing of God, may that country itself become a vast and splendid monument, not of oppression and terror, but of wisdom, of peace, and of liberty, upon which the world may gaze with admiration forever.

—Daniel Webster

91. THE NEW COLOSSUS

Not like the brazen giant of Greek fame,
With conquering limbs astride from land to land,
Here at our sea-washed, sunset gates shall stand
A mighty woman with a torch, whose flame
Is the imprisoned lightning, and her name
Mother of Exiles, From her beacon-hand
Glows world-wide welcome; her mild eyes command
The air-bridged harbor that twin cities frame.

"Keep, ancient lands, your storied pomp!" cries she
With silent lips. "Give me your tired, your poor,
Your huddled masses yearning to breathe free,
The wretched refuse of your teeming shore.
Send these, the homeless, tempest-tossed to me,
I lift my lamp beside the golden door!"

—Inscription on the Statue of Liberty,
written by Emma Lazarus

10
Inspiration for Daily Living

---

92. SHUT THE DOOR ON YESTERDAY

I've shut the door on yesterday,
  Its sorrows and mistakes;
I've locked within its gloomy walls
  Past failures and heartaches.

And now I throw the key away
  To seek another room,
And furnish it with hope and smiles,
  And every springtime bloom.

No thought shall enter this abode
  That has a hint of pain,
And every malice and distrust
  Shall never therein reign.

I've shut the door on yesterday
  And thrown the key away—
Tomorrow holds no doubt for me,
  Since I have found today.

—Author unknown

93. TROUBLE ME, LORD

Lord, trouble me over the littleness of my work for you;

Trouble me over my unholiness, my slowness to obey;

Trouble me over every lost hour, with time running out;

Trouble me over my sins and the sins of all people;

Trouble me over the effort and money I say I give to you but don't;

Trouble me over the times I say I will pray for someone but then forget;

Trouble me, O Lord, and let me keep faith in the midst of my troubles.

94. GOD'S PROMISES

God has not promised skies always blue,
Flower-strewn pathways all our life through;
God has not promised sun without rain,
Day without sorrow, peace without pain.

But God has promised strength for the day,
Rest for the labor, light for the way;
Grace for the trials, help from above,
Unfailing sympathy, undying love.

—Author unknown

95. I MET GOD IN THE MORNING

I met God in the morning
When my day was at its best
And His presence came like sunrise,
Like a glory in my breast.

All day long His presence lingered,
All day long He stayed with me;
And we sailed with perfect calmness
On a very troubled sea.

Other ships were blown and battered,
    Other ships were sore distressed;
But the winds that seemed to drive them
    Brought to us a peace and rest.

Then I thought of other mornings
    With a keen remorse of mind,
When I, too, had loosed the moorings
    With His presence left behind.

So I think I know the secret
    Learned from many a troubled way—
You must seek God in the morning
    If you want Him through the day.

—Ralph Cushman

96. THE REWARD OF PERSEVERANCE

There's no skill in easy sailing
    When the skies are clear and blue.
There's no joy in merely doing
    Things that anyone can do.

But there is great satisfaction
    That is mighty sweet to take
When you reach a destination
    That you thought you couldn't make.

—Author unknown

97. DON'T QUIT

When things go wrong, as they sometimes will,
When the road you're trudging seems all uphill,
When the funds are low and the debts are high
And you want to smile but you have to sigh;
When care is pressing you down a bit—
Rest if you must, but just don't quit.

Life is strange with its twists and turns,
As every one of us sometimes learns,
And many a person turns about
When he might have won had he stuck it out.

Don't give up, though the pace seems slow—
You may succeed with another blow.

Often the struggler has given up
When he might have captured the victor's cup,
And he learned too late when the night came down
How close he was to the golden crown.

Remember this truth when you start to doubt:
Success is failure turned inside out;
So stick to the fight when you're hardest hit—
It's when things seem worst that you mustn't quit.

—Author unknown

98. TWELVE SIMPLE RULES FOR HAPPINESS

1. Live a simple life. Do not plan too many things for each day. Be temperate and moderate in your lifestyle.

2. Spend less than you earn. This may be difficult to do, but it pays big dividends in contentment and peace of mind.

3. Think constructively. Store useful thoughts in your mind.

4. Cultivate a flexible disposition. Resist the tendency to want your own way. Try to see another person's point of view. Listen.

5. Be grateful. Begin each day with a prayer of thanksgiving for all your blessings.

6. Rule your moods. Your mental attitude is all-important in living at peace with others.

7. Give generously. Intelligent giving of your time, talents, personality, and money will bring great joy.

8. Work with right motives. Seek to grow in favor with God and man, seeking His will first in your life.

9. Be interested in others. As we serve others, we reap happiness as a by-product of a life of self-giving.

10. Make the most of today. Use it wisely so you may look back on it without regret.

11. Take time for a hobby. Time spent on leisure interests should bring you diversion and relaxation.

12. Stay close to God. Enduring happiness depends on continuing spiritual nourishment. As God's children, we have His promise of constant love and care.

99. A WORTHWHILE DAY

I count that day as wisely spent
In which I do some good
For someone who is far away
Or shares my neighborhood.

A day devoted to the deed
That lends a helping hand
And demonstrates a willingness
To care and understand.

I long to be of usefulness
In little ways and large
Without a selfish motive
And without the slightest charge.

Because in my philosophy
There never is a doubt
That all of us here on the earth
Must help each other out.

I feel that day is fruitful
And the time is worth the while
When I promote the happiness
Of one enduring smile.

—Author unknown

100. CALLED BACK BY THE SHEPHERD

One bad thing about sheep is that they have a tendency to stray. They put their heads down and start grazing without watching where they are going. They have such poor sense of direction that they will go right over a cliff. So if a sheep strays, it's generally in danger. The shepherd has to go out, find it, and restore it to the flock.

Aren't we often like that? We simply wander off from our Shepherd. But even though we may stray again and again, when we say, "Lord, forgive me," He brings us safely home (Ezek. 34:16).

The Bible says, "All we like sheep have gone astray; we have turned every one to his own way" (Isa. 53:6). But the Word of God also emphasizes that we can be "returned unto the shepherd" (1 Peter 2:25)—the eternal, loving God who calls us back to fellowship with Him.

101. BEGIN TODAY

So brief a time we have to stay
Along this dear, familiar way;
It seems to me we should be kind
To those whose lives touch yours and mine.

The hands that serve us every day,
Should we not help them while we may?
They are so kind that none can guess
How soon they'll cease our lives to bless.

The hearts that love us, who may know
How soon the long, long way must go.
Then might we not their faults forgive
And make them happy while they live?

So many faults in life there are
We need not go to seek them far;
But time is short and you and I
Might let the little faults go by.

And seek for what is true and fine
In those whose lives touch yours and mine;
This seems to me the better way.
Then why not, friend, begin today?

—Author unknown

102. A BRITTLE THING

A very brittle thing is speech;
Take care just how you bend it.

For anyone can make a break
But very few can mend it.

—Author unknown

103. A LITTLE MORE

A little more kindness and a little less creed,
A little more giving and a little less greed.
A little more smile and a little less frown,
A little less kicking a man when he's down.

A little more "we" and a little less "I,"
A little more laugh and a little less cry.
A little more flowers on the pathway of life;
And fewer on the grave at the end of the strife.

—Author unknown

104. IT MATTERS NOT

It matters not what others say
In ridicule or fun.
I want to live that I may hear
Him say to me, "Well done."

—Author unknown

105. PRAYER FOR A BUSY AGE

In the name of Jesus Christ, who was never in a hurry, we
pray, O God, that thou wilt slow us down, for we know
that we live too fast. With all of eternity before us, make
us take time to live—time to get acquainted with thee, time
to enjoy thy blessings, and time to know each other.
Through Jesus Christ our Lord. Amen.

—*Peter Marshall*

106. AT DAY'S END

Is anybody happier
* Because you passed his way?*
Does anyone remember
* That you spoke to him today?*
The day is almost over,
* And its toiling time is through;*
Is there anyone to utter
* Now a kindly word of you?*

Can you say tonight, in parting
* With the day that's slipping fast,*
That you helped a single brother
* Of the many that you passed?*
Is a single heart rejoicing
* Over what you did or said? —*
Does the man whose hopes were fading
* Now with courage look ahead?*

Did you waste the day or lose it?
* Was it well or sorely spent?*
Did you leave a trail of kindness
* Or a scar of discontent?*
As you close your eyes in slumber,
* Do you think that God will say,*
"You have earned one more tomorrow
* By the work you did today?"*

—John Hall

107. A GOODBYE THOUGHT

Now may the warming love of friends
* Surround you as you go*
Down paths of light and laughter
* Where the happy memories grow.*

—Helen Lowrie Marshall

108. ONE PRECIOUS DAY

I may never see tomorrow;
* There's no written guarantee,*

And things that happened yesterday
  Belong to history.
I cannot predict the future,
  And I cannot change the past.
I have just the present moment;
  I must treat it as my last.

I must use this moment wisely
  For it soon will pass away,
And be lost to me forever
  As a part of yesterday.
I must exercise compassion,
  Help the fallen to their feet,
Be a friend unto the friendless,
  Make an empty life complete.

I must make this moment precious,
  For it will not come again,
And I can never be content
  With things that might have been.
Kind words I fail to say this day
  May ever be unsaid,
For I know not how short may be
  The path that lies ahead.

The unkind things I do today
  May never be undone,
And friendships that I fail to win
  May nevermore be won.
I may not have another chance
  On bended knee to pray,
And thank my God with humble heart
  For giving me this day.

I may never see tomorrow,
  But this moment is my own.
It's mine to use or cast aside;
  The choice is mine alone.
I have just this precious moment
  In the sunlight of today,
Where the dawning of tomorrow
  Meets the dusk of yesterday.

—Author unknown

109. JUST A MINUTE

I have only just a minute,
Only sixty seconds in it;
Forced upon me, can't refuse it,
Didn't seek it, didn't choose it.
But it's up to me to use it,
I must suffer if I lose it,
Give account if I abuse it.
Just a tiny little minute—
But eternity is in it.

—Author unknown

110. GIVE ME A FRIEND

Give me a friend and I'll shuffle along:
My vision may vanish, my dream may go wrong;
My wealth I may lose, or my money may spend;
But I'll walk right along if you give me a friend.

Give me a friend and my youth may depart,
But still I'll be young in the house of my heart;
Yes, I'll go on laughing right on to the end,
Whatever the years, if you give me a friend.

—Author unknown

111. THE THINGS WE LEAVE BEHIND

Out of this life I shall never take
Things of silver and gold I make.
All that I cherish and hoard away,
After I leave, on the earth must stay.

Though I have toiled for a painting rare,
To hang on the wall, I must leave it there;
Though I call it mine and I boast its worth,
I must give it up when I leave the earth.

All that I gather and all that I keep
I must leave behind when I fall asleep.
And I often wonder what I shall own
In that other life when I pass alone.

Shall the Great Judge learn when my task is through,
That my spirit had gathered some riches, too?
Or shall at the last it be mine to find
That all I had worked for, I left behind.

—Author unknown

112. RUNGS ON THE LADDER OF ACHIEVEMENT

100%—I did
90%—I will
80%—I can
70%—I think I can
60%—I might
50%—I think I might
40%—What is it?
30%—I wish I could
20%—I don't know how
10%—I can't
0%—I won't

113. THE CHRISTIAN'S CREED

Let me be a little kinder,
*   Let me be a little blinder*
To the faults of those around me;
*   Let me praise a little more;*
Let me be, when I am weary,
*   Just a little bit more cheery;*
Let me serve a little better
*   Those that I am striving for.*

Let me be a little braver
*   When temptation bids me waver;*
Let me strive a little harder
*   To be all that I should be.*
Let me be a little meeker
*   With my brother who is weaker;*
Let me think more of my neighbor
*   And a little less of me.*

—Author unknown

73

11
Interpersonal Relationships

---

114. TIPS ON HOW TO GET ALONG WITH PEOPLE

1. Keep chains on your tongue and always say less than you think. Cultivate a pleasant, persuasive voice. How you say it often counts more than what you say.

2. Make promises sparingly and keep them faithfully.

3. Never let an opportunity pass to say a kind word to somebody. Praise good work, regardless of who did it. If correction is needed, criticize helpfully, never in a destructive manner.

4. Be genuinely interested in others. Let everyone you meet feel that you regard him or her as a person of importance.

5. Be cheerful. Keep the corners of your mouth turned up. Hide your pains, worries, and disappointments under a smile.

6. Keep an open mind on all controversial questions. Discuss without arguing. It is possible to disagree and yet be friendly.

7. Never engage in gossip. Make it a rule to say nothing about another unless it is something good.

8. Be careful of other people's feelings. Laughing at another's expense is rarely worth the effort, and it may hurt when least expected.

9. Pay no attention to cutting remarks that others may make about you. Learn to live above such comments.

10. Don't be too anxious about your rights and having favors repaid. Let the satisfaction of helping others serve as its own reward.

115. PROBING QUESTIONS TO ASK YOURSELF

1. Am I so critical that I see only a person's failures and not his good points?

2. Am I so childish that people must handle me gently lest I be offended?

3. Am I mature enough to handle hurts and disappointments without feeling mistreated and making everyone else miserable?

4. Do I hurt people while boasting, "I believe in saying what I think?"

5. Can I be completely trusted with confidential information?

6. Am I guilty of making sarcastic remarks about the success of others?

7. Am I big enough to admit when I am wrong, or do I seek to excuse myself by blaming others?

8. Do I excuse my sins while self-righteously condemning those of others?

9. Are others uplifted and encouraged through their association with me?

10. Do I follow after peace, or do my words and actions promote strife?

11. When the good name of an outstanding person is undermined, do I silently rejoice, "That is what I thought all the time"?

12. When a discourtesy is shown me, do I brood over it and determine to get even?

If you answered "Yes" to any of these questions, you still have some room for growth in your Christian life.

116. HOW TO BUILD STRONG FRIENDSHIPS

1. Permit your friends to be themselves. Accept them as they are. Accept their imperfections and individuality; don't feel threatened if their opinions and tastes sometimes differ from yours.

2. Give each other space. We are entitled to our private feelings and thoughts. Someone who tries to invade the inner space of a friend risks destroying that relationship.

3. Be ready to give and receive. Be eager to help but be able to ask for help as well. Don't be over-demanding or let yourself be used.

4. Make your advice constructive. When a friend needs to talk, listen without interruption. If advice is asked for, be positive and supportive.

5. Be loyal and faithful. This translates into being with your friend in bad times as well as good ones. It means honoring confidences. It means neither disparaging a friend in his absence nor allowing others to do so.

6. Give praise and encouragement. Tell your friends what you like about them and how thankful you are for their presence in your life. Delight in their talents, and applaud their successes.

7. Be honest, but be aware of those things that are better left unsaid.

8. Treat friends as equals. In true friendship there is no room for such childish behavior as showing off how smart and successful you are.

9. Trust your friends. Make the effort to believe in their intrinsic goodness.

10. Be willing to risk. One of the obstacles to a close friendship is the fear of rejection and hurt. But unless we dare to love others, we condemn ourselves to lives of isolation and loneliness.

117. WE REALLY DO NEED ONE ANOTHER

During a hike in the woods, a troop of Boy Scouts came across an abandoned railroad track. Each, in turn, tried walking the rails, but eventually lost his balance and tumbled off.

Suddenly two of the boys, after considerable whispering, bet that they could both walk the entire length of the track without falling off. Challenged to make good their boast, the two boys jumped up on opposite rails, extended their hands to balance each other, and walked the entire section of track with no difficulty whatever.

This, in a nutshell, is an important principle of life. The day of the hermit, the lone wolf, and the self-made man is gone forever. Made in the image of God, we are so constituted that we thrive on partnership, companionship, and fellowship. We do things better, we produce more, and we live happier by helping one another. The person who lends a helping hand discovers that he benefits himself as he helps the other. When we don't support one another, our lives begin to get offtrack. We really do need one another.

—*Mike Clayton*

118. THE PERSON DOWN THE ROAD

In thirty, forty, or fifty years you will meet a person down the road. Whether that someone is kind and gentle or

77

selfish and demanding depends on what you do today. If you live only in terms of what you can get out of life, this person will be crabby, self-centered, and spiteful. But if you open your life to others and live as a giver, this person will be kind, open, and generous.

This somebody whom you will meet down the road is you. The person you will be tomorrow depends on the life you live today. Make sure the person you are becoming is someone you'll enjoy being around for the rest of your life.

119. THE FINE ART OF FORGIVENESS

The art of forgiving those who wrong us is one of the greatest spiritual graces. Here are some principles of forgiveness that are based on the teachings of the Bible:

1. Remember how often God has forgiven you when you did not deserve His forgiveness.

2. List the blessings and the mercies which you have received from the hand of God and which you did not deserve.

3. Remember that the Spirit of Christ lives in you and that He will enable you to forgive, even as Christ forgave those who wronged Him.

4. Begin now to pray earnestly for God to bless the person who has wronged you.

5. Make a special effort to surprise the person who has wronged you with some act of kindness or thoughtfulness—a birthday card, an anniversary gift, a letter.

6. Repeat slowly and thoughtfully this phrase from the Lord's Prayer, "Forgive us our debts as we forgive our debtors."

12
Jesus Christ
His Mission and Message

---

120. A DEFINITION OF GRACE

God's

Riches

At

Christ's

Expense

121. THE WONDER OF THE EMPTY TOMB

The ancient world boasted of seven wonders: the pyramids of Egypt; the hanging gardens of Babylon; the temple of the goddess Diana at Ephesus; the lighthouse at Alexandria, Egypt; the Colossus (a huge bronze statue) in the harbor at Rhodes; the statue of the pagan god Zeus at Olympia, Greece; and the tomb of the Persian king Halicarnassus.

Of all these ancient wonders, only the pyramids are still standing. All the others have crumbled, along with the ancient world powers whose accomplishments they memorialized. But another wonder from the ancient world is still very much alive today. This wonder is more significant than all seven of these ancient landmarks put together. This is the wonder of the empty tomb of Jesus at Jerusalem.

When the body of Jesus was placed in the tomb, the forces of evil seemed to be victorious at last. But Jesus was raised on the third day. His resurrection proved that He was more powerful than sin and death and all the other negative forces that Satan uses against us.

Wonder of wonders, Jesus lives! And His dynamic power is available to all who place their faith and trust in Him.

122. THE BEST FORM

God said, "Let us form man in our image."

The world says, "Man must conform to our image."

The devil says, "I will deform man by sin."

Education says, "Let us inform man by knowledge."

Society says, "We will reform man by culture."

Jesus says, "I will transform man by my love."

123. WHAT JESUS HAS DONE FOR HIS PEOPLE

He descended to earth that we might ascend to heaven (John 6:38; 14:3).

He became poor that we might become rich (2 Cor. 8:9; James 2:5).

He was born that we might be born again (John 1:14; 3:3).

He became a servant that we might be sons (Gal. 4:6–7; Phil. 2:7).

He had no home that we might have a home in heaven (Matt. 8:20; John 14:2).

He was hungry that we might be fed (Matt. 4:2; John 6:50).

He was thirsty that we might drink of the springs of salvation (Isa. 12:3; John 19:28).

He was made weary that we might find rest (Matt. 11:29; John 4:6).

He was stripped that we might be clothed (Matt. 27:28; 2 Cor. 5:4).

He was forsaken that we might be accepted (Matt. 27:46; Heb. 13:5).

He was sad that we might be glad (Isa. 53:3; Phil. 4:4).

He was bound that we might go free (Matt. 27:2; John 8:32–36).

He was made sin that we might be made righteous (2 Cor. 5:21).

He died that we might live (John 5:24–25; 19:33).

He will come down that we may be caught up into heaven (1 Thess. 4:16–17).

124. THE CROSS IN MY POCKET

I carry a cross in my pocket—
  A simple reminder to me
Of the fact that I am a Christian,
  No matter where I may be.

This little cross is not magic
  Nor is it a good luck charm;
It isn't meant to protect me
  From every physical harm.

It's not for identification
  For all the world to see;
It's simply an understanding
  Between my Savior and me.

When I put my hand in my pocket
  To bring out a coin or key,
The cross is there to remind me
  Of the price He paid for me.

It reminds me, too, to be thankful
  For my blessings day by day,
And to strive to serve Him better
  In all that I do and say.

It's also a daily reminder
  Of the peace and comfort I share
With all who know my Master
  And give themselves to His care.

So I carry the cross in my pocket,
  Reminding no one but me
That Jesus Christ is Lord of my life—
  If only I'll let Him be.

—Author unknown

125. IF JESUS CAME TO YOUR HOUSE

If Jesus came to your house to spend a day or two,
If He should show up unannounced, I wonder what you'd do?
Would you have to change your clothes before you let Him in,
Or hide some books and put the Bible where they'd been?
Would you be glad to have Him meet your very closest friends,
Or would you hope they stay away until His visit ends?
Would you be glad to have Him stay forever on and on,
Or would you sigh with great relief when He at last was gone?
It might be interesting to know the things that you would do,
If Jesus came in person to spend some time with you.

—Author unknown

13
Mother's Day Messages

126. IT TAKES A MOTHER

It takes a mother's love to make a house a home,
A place to be remembered, no matter where we roam.
It takes a mother's patience to bring a child up right
And her courage and her cheerfulness to make a dark day
*   bright.*

It takes a mother's kindness to forgive us when we err,
To sympathize in trouble and bow her head in prayer.
It takes a mother's wisdom to recognize our needs
And give us reassurance by her loving words and deeds.

It takes a mother's endless faith, her confidence and trust,
To guide us through the pitfalls of selfishness and lust.
And that is why in all this world there can never be another
Who will fulfill God's purposes as completely as a mother.

—Author unknown

127. MEMORIES OF MOTHER

She carried me under her heart, loved me before I was born, took God's hand and walked through the "valley of shadows" that I might live.

She bathed me when I was helpless, clothed me when I was naked, fed me when I was hungry, rocked me to sleep when I was weary, and sang to me with the voice of an angel.

She held my hand when I learned to walk, suffered with my sorrow, laughed with my joy, glowed with my triumph, and while I knelt at her side, she taught me to pray.

She was a loyal friend when others failed. Through all the days of my youth, she gave me strength for my weakness, courage for my despair, and hope for my hopeless heart.

She prayed for me whether the day was flooded with sunshine or saddened by shadows. I can never repay the debt I owe to my mother.

128. TO MOTHER, ON MOTHER'S DAY

For all the things you've been to me,
My guardian and my guide;
For truths you have so gently taught
And all the tears you've dried.
For faith and understanding
When I faltered on my way,
I owe you more thanks, Mother,
Than words can ever say.

So on this day that's set aside
Especially for you,
I send a wish for happiness
In everything you do.
May each hour bring you pleasure
Every day of every year—
For all the things you've been to me,
I love you, Mother dear.

—Author unknown

129. PRAYER FOR MOTHER'S DAY

On this day of sacred memories, our Father, we thank you for our mothers who gave us life, who surrounded us early and late with love and care, whose prayers on our behalf still cling around the throne of grace, a haunting perfume of love's petitions.

Help us, their children, to be more worthy of their love. We know that no sentimentality on this one day, no material gifts—no flowers or boxes of candy—can atone for our neglect during the rest of the year. So in the days ahead, may our love speak to the hearts who know love best—by kindness, by compassion, by simple courtesy and daily thoughtfulness.

Bless her whose name we whisper before you, and keep her in your perfect peace. Through Jesus Christ our Lord. Amen.

—Peter Marshall

130. HOW MOTHER'S DAY BEGAN

Anna M. Jarvis (1864–1948) first suggested the national observance of an annual day honoring all mothers because she had loved her own mother so dearly. At a memorial service for her mother on May 10, 1908, Miss Jarvis gave a carnation (her mother's favorite flower) to each person who attended. Within the next few years the idea of a day to honor mothers gained popularity, and Mother's Day was observed in a number of large cities in the United States.

On May 9, 1914, by an act of Congress, President Woodrow Wilson proclaimed the second Sunday in May as Mother's Day. He established the day as a time for "public expression of our love and reverence for the mothers of our country." By then it had become customary to wear a white carnation to honor deceased mothers and a red flower to honor the living—a custom that continues to this day.

131. THE UNCROWNED QUEEN

When God would save a world from sin,
He chose with mothers to begin;
And, through a virgin mother birth
To bring good will to men on earth.

When Christ the way of life would tell,
A woman listened by a well;
When He was tired and needed rest,
Two women honored Him as guest;
He caused a maid to walk again
And raised a widow's son at Nain.

When Christ was hanging on a cross,
A mother's heart most felt the loss;
Two women were the first to see
At dawn, the empty sepulchre;
The resurrected Christ was seen
At first by Mary Magdalene.

A mother's love will stand by you
When other friends have proved untrue;
She'll round your bed her vigil keep
While other eyes are closed in sleep.
She'll cleave to you till life shall end
And be your faithful, loving friend.

Our mothers steer the ship of state;
'Tis they who make the nation great.
Our nation will be bad or good,
According to its motherhood.
And back of all great men is seen
The image of an uncrowned queen.

—Author unknown

132. PORTRAIT OF A MOTHER

A mother can be almost any size or any age, but she won't admit to anything over thirty. She has soft hands and smells good. A mother likes new dresses, music, a clean house, her children's kisses, an automatic washer, and Daddy.

A mother doesn't like having her children sick, muddy feet, temper tantrums, loud noise, or bad report cards. She can read a thermometer (much to the amazement of Daddy) and, like magic, can kiss a hurt away. She can also bake good cakes and pies, but she likes to see her children eat vegetables.

A mother can stuff a fat baby into a snowsuit in seconds and can kiss a little face and make it smile. She is underpaid, has long hours, and gets very little rest. She worries too much about her children. And no matter how old they are, she still likes to think of them as her little children.

A mother is the guardian of the family, the queen, the tender hand of love. She is the best friend anyone ever had. A mother is love.

133. MEMORIES OF MOTHER

As long ago we carried to your knees
The tales and treasures of eventful days,
Knowing no deed too humble for your praise,
Nor any gift too trivial to please.

So still we bring with older smiles and tears,
What gifts we may to claim the old, dear right;
Your faith beyond the silence and the night;
Your love still close and watching through the years.

—Author unknown

14
New Year's Messages

---

134. PROMISES FOR THE NEW YEAR

This year why not make some promises rather than resolutions for the new year? The following list should get you started.

Promise to be so strong that nothing can disturb your peace of mind.

Promise to make all your friends feel that there is something special about them.

Promise to look at the sunny side of everything and make your optimism come true.

Promise to think only of the best, to work only for the best, and to make the best come true.

Promise to be just as enthusiastic about the success of others as you are about your own.

Promise to forget the mistakes of the past and press on to greater achievements in the future.

Promise to wear a cheerful expression at all times and to give every person you meet a smile.

Promise to give so much effort to the improvement of yourself that you have no time to criticize others.

Promise to be too big for worry, too noble for anger, too strong for fear, and too happy to permit the presence of trouble in your life.

135. REQUESTS FOR THE NEW YEAR

What shall I ask for the coming year?
What shall my watchword be?
What should thou do for me, dear Lord?
What can I do for thee?

Lord, I would ask for a holy year,
Spent in thy perfect will.
Help me to walk in thy very steps;
Help me to please thee still.

Lord, I would ask for a trustful year,
Give me thy faith divine,
Taking my full inheritance,
Making thy fulness mine!

Lord, I would ask for a year of love;
O let me love thee best!
Give me the love that faileth not
Beneath the hardest test.

Lord, I would ask for a year of prayer,
Teach me to walk with thee;
Breathe in my heart the Spirit's prayer;
Pray thou thy prayer in me!

Lord, I would ask for the dying world,
Stretch forth thy mighty hand;
Thy truth proclaim, thy power display
This year in every land.

Lord, I would ask for a year of joy;
Thy peace, thy joy divine,
Springing undimmed through all the days
Be thy days of shade or shine.

Lord, I ask for a year of hope,
Looking for thee to come,
And hastening on that year of years
That brings us Christ and Home.

—Author unknown

136. A PRAYER FOR THE NEW YEAR

Father of mercies, teach us today and every day of the year to see in all that surrounds us occasions for praise and thanksgiving to you: When we behold the beauty of the earth's garments and of a surrendered life; when we wonder at the power of a storm and of your transforming love; when we listen to the happy laughter of children and to the promises of your Word. When life gets so dreary that we find it difficult to praise you, remind us of the working of your hands in every corner of the universe.

Help us, dear Lord, to commit our lives to the noble causes for which Jesus Christ lived and died. Help us to stand for the right rather than the easy; to search for truth rather than popularity; to fight for the welfare of people rather than institutions; and to love all people rather than seek to be loved by all people.

Help each person in his or her need. Deliver us from the guilt and love of our sins. Through Jesus Christ our Lord. Amen.

137. STEP BY STEP

He does not lead me year by year,
Nor even day by day;
But step by step my path unfolds,
My Lord directs my way.

Tomorrow's plans I do not know;
I only know this minute.
But He will say, "This is the way,
By faith now walk ye in it."

And I am glad that it is so,
   Today's enough to bear;
And when tomorrow comes, His grace
   Shall far exceed its care.

What need to worry then, or fret?
   The God who gave His Son
Holds all my moments in His hand
   And gives them one by one.

—Author unknown

138. JONATHAN EDWARDS' NEW YEAR'S RESOLUTIONS

Resolved:

To live with all my might while I do live.

Never to lose one moment of time, to improve it in the most profitable way I can.

Never to do anything which I should despise or think meanly of in another.

Never to do anything out of revenge.

Never to do anything which I would be afraid to do if it were the last hour of my life.

139. SAILING INTO THE NEW YEAR

God built and launched this year for you;
   Upon the bridge you stand;
It's your ship, aye, your own ship,
   And you are in command.
Just what the twelve months' trip will do
   Rests wholly, solely, friend, with you.

Your logbook kept from day to day
   My friend, what will it show?
Have you on your appointed way
   Made progress, yes or no?
The log will tell, like guiding star,
   The sort of captain that you are.

For weal or woe this year is yours;
  Your ship is on life's sea
Your acts, as captain, must decide
  Whichever it shall be;
So now in starting on your trip,
  Ask God to help you sail your ship.

—Author unknown

15
The Pastor and
His Work

140. THE PERFECT PASTOR

At last we have developed a model for a perfect pastor that will suit everyone! He's guaranteed to please any church that calls him. He preaches exactly fourteen minutes. He condemns sin, but never hurts anyone's feelings.

He works from 9:00 in the morning until 11:00 at night, in every type of work—from preaching to custodial services. His salary is $60.00 a week. He wears good clothes, buys good books, has a nice family, drives a nice car, and gives $30.00 a week to the church.

This perfect pastor is thirty years old, but he has been preaching for thirty-five years. He is tall, short, thin, heavyset, and very handsome. His hair is parted in the middle, with the left side dark and straight and the right side light and wavy. He has a burning desire to work with young people, and spends all his time with the older folks.

He smiles all the time with a straight face because he has a sense of humor that keeps him seriously dedicated to his work. Although he makes ten calls a day on church members, ten on the unchurched, and five on those in the hospital, he is always available for telephone calls in the office.

141. SIX WAYS TO HELP YOUR PASTOR HELP YOUR CHURCH

1. Let him know of spiritual needs. When sickness or death strikes, the pastor may not hear of it until it's too late—unless some thoughtful person lets him know.

2. Attend worship consistently. This will encourage him greatly in his work.

3. Carry your share of the church load. A minister who has to push everything soon becomes weary. Take some initiative yourself in performing your duties in the church.

4. Inform your pastor of new people in town or on your block. Every pastor wants to visit new people, but unless you keep him posted about newcomers, he may miss them.

5. Share the visitation. No minister can make all the calls that need to be made.

6. Be his friend. A pastor is also human. Your friendship will be a big encouragement to him in the Lord's work.

142. A MESSAGE TO THE PASTOR'S WIFE

As pastor's wife you're looked upon
By those who congregate
To see if you appear just right
Or come to meetings late.

And people always see your faults
And criticize your ways
Because you're in the public eye—
The object of its gaze.

But don't you worry about us folk,
And what we think or say;

Just let the Lord love all of us
And love through you today.

Nor don't you try to please us all,
For that will never do!
Just keep on satisfying Him
And He will see you through.

—Author unknown

16
Prayer

---

143. THE REAL MEANING OF PRAYER

1. Prayer is not God doing things for us; prayer is God helping us to do things for ourselves.

2. Prayer does not change circumstances; prayer changes us.

3. Prayer is not escape; prayer is conquest.

4. Prayer is not so much talking to God as listening to God. Prayer is not so much telling God what we want Him to do as it is listening to see what He wants us to do.

—William Barclay

144. FAR AND NEAR

Prayer is a powerful telescope
That lets the eye see far
To the star of things as they ought to be
From the land of things as they are.

And prayer, too, is a microscope
That lets the eye see near
And count the worth of things of earth
The heart holds close and dear.

—Author unknown

145. NEEDED: MORE PRAY-ERS

The church has many organizers but few agonizers in prayer; many who pay but few who pray; many resters but few wrestlers; many who are enterprising but few who are interceding.

Two requirements for a dynamic Christian life are vision and passion, and both of these are generated in the prayer closet. The ministry of preaching is open to a few, but the ministry of prayer is open to every child of God.

Tithes may build a church, but tears will give it life. That is the difference between the modern church and the early church. Our emphasis is on paying, while theirs was on praying.

146. TEN GUIDELINES FOR EFFECTIVE PRAYER

1. Set aside a few minutes every day. Do not say anything; simply practice thinking about God. This will make your mind spiritually receptive.

2. Then pray orally, using simple, natural words. Tell God everything that is on your mind. Do not think you must use stereotyped, pious phrases. Talk to God in your own natural language. He understands.

3. Pray as you go about the business of the day. Utter minute prayers by closing your eyes to shut out the world and concentrating briefly on God's presence. The more you do this every day, the nearer you will feel God's presence.

4. Do not always ask for something when you pray. Spend most of your prayer time giving thanks for God Himself and His blessings.

5. Pray with the belief that sincere prayers can reach out and surround your loved ones with God's love and protection.

6. Never use negative thoughts in prayer. Only positive thoughts get results.

7. Always express willingness to accept God's will. Ask for what you want, but be willing to take what God gives you. It may be better than what *you* ask for.

8. Practice the attitude of putting everything in God's hands. Ask for the ability to do your best and to leave the results to God.

9. Pray for people you do not like or who have mistreated you. Resentment is guaranteed to short-circuit spiritual power.

10. Make a list of people for whom to pray. The more you pray for others, the more positive results you will note from your prayers.

17
Sentence Sermons

147. THE FUTURE: A DEFINITION

The future is that time when you'll wish you had done what you aren't doing now.

148. KEEP IT BURNING

It is much easier to keep the fire burning than to rekindle it after it has gone out.

149. THE FUTILE VISIT

God often visits us, but most of the time we are not at home.

150. SLAPPING AND SWALLOWING

Just remember that the person who is slapping you on the back may be trying to get you to swallow everything he tells you.

151. GREAT EXPECTATIONS

Too many Christians expect a million-dollar answer to a ten-cent prayer.

152. THE HARD WORK PRINCIPLE

If you want a place in the sun, you have to expect some blisters.

153. A SURE THING

To do the right thing is the only investment that never fails.

154. USABILITY ESSENTIAL

God doesn't look for great ability as much as He looks for *usability*.

155. LONG ENOUGH

Life may be short, but it gives most of us time to outlive our good intentions.

156. REAL KNOWLEDGE

It's what we learn after we think we know it all that really counts.

157. DON'T INTERRUPT

People who say it's impossible should not interrupt those who are managing to get it done.

158. NEGATIVE THINKING

If you keep on saying things are going to be bad, you stand a good chance of becoming a prophet.

159. NO HARM DONE

The devil is quite willing for a person to profess Christianity—as long as he doesn't put it into practice.

160. TACT DEFINED

Tact is the ability to close your mouth before someone else wants to.

161. FRUITFUL TROUBLE

One good thing about trouble is that it gives you something to talk about besides the weather.

162. A REAL FRIEND

A true friend is a person who remembers your birthday but forgets how many you've had.

163. THE POWER OF ACTION

The smallest deed is better than the greatest intention.

164. MOTIVATION SHORTAGE

Most of us are not overworked; we are just undermotivated.

165. A MEANINGFUL PRAYER

Lord, I do not ask for a faith that will move mountains. I pray, Lord, for enough faith to move me.

166. PUT YESTERDAY BEHIND

Never let yesterday use up too much of today.

167. THE UNIVERSAL DESIRE

Most of us want the same thing out of life—more than we deserve.

168. THE JUMPING GAME

Ever wonder why we don't jump at opportunities as quickly as we jump to conclusions?

169. THE SECRET OF GIVING

If a person first gives himself to the Lord, all other giving is easy.

170. A USELESS ACTIVITY

No matter how long you nurse a grudge, it won't get better.

171. WHAT TO DO WITH WORRIES

Every night when you go to bed, turn all your worries over to God. After all, He's going to be up all night anyway!

172. SUCCESS: A REALISTIC VIEW

If at first you don't succeed—you're about average.

173. A POSITIVE "I"

"I must do something" will always solve more problems than "Something must be done."

174. GAINING EXPERIENCE

The best way to move mountains is to begin with molehills and work your way up.

175. ARTFUL CONVERSATION

Diplomacy is the art of telling others they have open minds instead of holes in their heads.

176. A FATAL MISTAKE

The biggest mistake an employee can make is to assume he's working for someone else.

177. PATIENCE: A DEFINITION

Patience is the ability to count down when you want to blast off.

178. STAYING POWER

Remember that an oak tree is nothing but an acorn that held its own ground.

179. TEMPER YOUR EXPECTATIONS

The secret of being happy ever after is not to be after too much.

180. OPPORTUNITY MANUFACTURING

The wise person will make more opportunities than he finds.

181. LEARNING FROM MISTAKES

All some people learn from their mistakes is to blame them on others.

182. GOOD ADVICE

If you ask enough people, you'll always find someone who advises you to do exactly what you planned to do in the first place.

183. HOW TO FAIL

A proven formula for failure is to try to please everybody.

184. WATCH YOUR PRAYERS

Don't pray for rain if you intend to complain about the mud.

185. NO TALENT NECESSARY

You don't have to be much of a musician to toot your own horn.

186. HOW TO MULTIPLY YOUR TROUBLES

A sure way to multiply your troubles is to brood over them.

187. THE SMELL OF GOOD LUCK

Good luck often has the lingering odor of perspiration.

188. LIFE FROM THE SIDELINES

It's always easy to see both sides of an issue you're not particularly concerned about.

189. GET READY!

Take things as they come—if you can handle them that fast.

18
Stewardship and Church Finance

190. JESUS TALKED ABOUT MONEY

Some people find it surprising that Jesus talked so much about money during His earthly ministry. Here are a few of the things He taught us about how to use money and material things:

1. Jesus taught us to concentrate on heavenly treasures: "Do not lay up for yourselves treasures on earth, where moth and rust corrupt and where thieves break in and steal; but lay up for yourselves treasures in heaven, where neither moth nor rust destroys and where thieves do not break in and steal" (Matt. 6:19–20).

2. Jesus taught that people would be happier giving rather than receiving: "It is more blessed to give than to receive" (Acts 20:35).

3. Jesus warned that material things could become a hindrance to spiritual growth: "How hard it is for those who have riches to enter the kingdom of God!" (Mark 10:23).

4. Jesus declared that we do not live on material things alone, no matter how much wealth we have: "A man's life

does not consist in the abundance of things he possesses" (Luke 12:15).

5. Jesus instructed us to have pure motives for our giving: "Take heed that you do not do your charitable deeds before men. . . . I say to you, they have their reward" (Matt. 6:1–2).

6. Jesus cautioned against worry over material things, and called on us to trust God to provide for our needs: "Do not worry about your life, what you will eat or what you will drink; nor your body, what you will put on. Is not life more than food and the body than clothing?" (Matt. 6:25).

Yes, Jesus talked a lot about money. We need His attitude toward material things. Money was intended to be our servant, not our master.

191. WHAT A HORRIBLE DREAM!

I dreamed that the Lord took my weekly contribution to the church, multiplied it by ten, and turned this amount into my weekly income. In no time I lost all my furniture and had to give up my automobile. Why, I couldn't even make a house payment! What can a person do on $10.00 a week?

Suppose the Lord took your offering and multiplied it by ten and made that your weekly income. How much would you earn? This question might give you some fresh insights into the stewardship needs of the church.

192. A STEWARDSHIP PARABLE

And behold, a certain man went down with a friend to a place where people like to eat. And there the two of them dined sumptuously. And when they finished eating, the waitress brought the men a bill. And in the sight of his friend the man placed beside his plate a certain sum of coins. "What does this sum of money beside your plate mean?" the friend inquired.

"It is but a tip, a customary percentage of the sum of the bill," the man answered.

The friend said to himself: "How strange this is! This man has been served for a few minutes by the waitress, and behold, he gives to her 15 percent of the bill. All his life he has received this world's goods from his heavenly father, yet he is offended that God should ask of him a tenth part—a tithe—of his increase. Can it be that he holds this waitress, a stranger, in greater esteem than his heavenly Father?"

193. AN UNUSED ENVELOPE SPEAKS OUT

Look inside this year's church envelope box. If you find me there, I can tell you a story. I'll remind you of the Sunday when you missed Sunday school and church. Just check the date written on me. I can't tell you why you missed. You'll have to think back to remember. Did you have a good reason? Notice I said reason, not excuse.

I was designed to hold any amount you want to give. I look much better when I am fat with a love offering than I do flat, unsealed, and useless. I have no power over myself. I am your servant. I had counted so much on going to the Lord's treasury. Now I shall never go.

I can tell you about your spiritual life, too. When I am used, I speak of an honest heart. I could have been filled and taken to church later even though you missed the Sunday that was stamped on me.

Because I am still unused, I speak of limits placed on God's work. Do you hear the cry of children without parents, do you see the sick without care, the ignorant untaught, the church not built, the Bibles not sent, the gospel not preached, the lost without hope? I could have helped meet these needs if only I had been used.

I am empty and heartbroken. Let me touch your conscience and stir your heart. Please don't let this happen in future weeks to my friends who are still here with me in the box.

194. YOUR SUPPORT CAN MAKE THE DIFFERENCE

Of all human experiences, being forgotten and forsaken must hurt the most. Think of an unwanted child, with parents who don't care. Can anyone measure the loneliness a little child like this must endure? The unhappy days without love?

What is it like to live in a forgotten land, where each day is a struggle to stay alive? Where hunger pits man against child. Where the human spirit fights for one more day to live while the body begs to die. A wretched life of fear and isolation. Abandoned, forsaken, forgotten by people living in lavish luxury.

A church can be forgotten. It can struggle in heartache and despair when numbers, in apathy, choose not to give it their support. When this happens, a church battles to stay alive, wasting time counting pennies instead of doing God's work. And the children and the hungry are forgotten.

But when a church is remembered, God's work faces a future filled with cheerful, happy, bright days. And the children and the hungry also feel this promise. Your financial support can make the difference.

19
Sunday School Attendance and Support

---

195. WHEN A SUNDAY SCHOOL TEACHER IS SUCCESSFUL

A Sunday school teacher is successful . . .

 . . . When his pupils are becoming his closest friends rather than Sunday morning acquaintances.

 . . . When he is able to instill in them high ideals for Christian living.

 . . . When he can look his class straight in the eye because he knows that he is hiding nothing from them.

 . . . When he sets aside a portion of each day for spiritual growth through prayer and Bible reading.

 . . . When he is unwilling for a single pupil in his class to remain unsaved.

196. TEN PRINCIPLES OF SUNDAY SCHOOL GROWTH

We would see the number of persons involved in Bible study increase dramatically in one year if we prayerfully and consistently did the following things:

1. Keep the class organized. If you do not have class officers, elect or appoint them immediately.

2. Use these officers. Do not do all the work yourself. People like to be needed and utilized. Get them involved.

3. Have a regular program of weekly visitation. Set a time when most of your class can visit.

4. Go after prospects for your class. After a few months, classes tend to become self-satisfied. New people coming into the class bring life and vitality.

5. Teach the Bible. Prepare thoroughly for the lesson. Do not waste time by talking about ball games and current events too long. People are anxious to know what *God* has to say.

6. Have regular class meetings. Meet in the homes of members. Use these home meetings to get to know your members.

7. Keep a roll of your class and pray daily for yourself as a teacher, your members (by name), and prospects.

8. Cooperate with the church. You are a part of a great body. The best classes are not independent units but workers with the rest of the church for Christ.

9. Improve your abilities by attending a training class. Every teacher can become a better teacher by examining new methods of teaching and leading.

10. Ask the Holy Spirit to fill and use you. God's work can only be done by God's people through God's power.

197. HAND IN HAND, A CHILD AND I

Dear Lord, I do not ask
  That thou shouldst give me some high work of thine,
Some noble calling or some wondrous task.
  Give me a little hand to hold in mine;
Give me a little child to point the way
  Over the strange, sweet path that leads to thee;

Give me a little voice to teach to pray;
Give me two shining eyes thy face to see.

The only crown I ask, dear Lord, to wear is this—
That I may teach a little child. I do not ask
That I should ever stand among the wise, the worthy, or the
great;
I only ask that softly, hand in hand,
A child and I may enter at thy gate.

—Author unknown

198. WHEN, O WHEN . . .

"When, O when, can I break the rule
And no longer go to Sunday school?"
This is the question I asked one day,
And my teacher answered this funny way:

"When the water is gone from all the seas,
And pigs wear hats and coats and pants;
When pussy cats grow on the pumpkin vine,
And three times seven is twenty-nine;
When black is white and red is green
And children's faces are always clean;
When boys and girls no longer eat
Cookies and cakes and candies sweet—
Then, O then, you can break the rule
And no longer go to Sunday school!"

—Author unknown

199. A TEACHER'S CODE OF ETHICS

As a teacher in my church, I will do my best:

—To approach my task each Sunday with a prepared heart and a reverent attitude.

—To make every effort to grow in the grace of the Lord Jesus Christ and to lead my pupils to do the same.

—To contact absentees promptly, personally, and persistently.

—To set an example in attendance, punctuality, and stewardship.

—To make my instruction personal and practical, adapting the lesson to the needs of my class members.

—To make a conscientious effort to win every pupil and to help him or her live as a Christian disciple.

—To cooperate gladly with my pastor, Sunday school director, and other officers.

—To use every possible method of improving my teaching.

—To esteem Christ first, others second, and myself last.

200. PARABLE OF THE APATHETIC ADULTS

Once upon a time there was a nominating committee looking for teachers for their young people, children, and preschoolers for the new Sunday school year. And some adults said, "I don't want to leave the sweet fellowship and study in my adult class." (But the drug pusher on the street said, "Not even the threat of jail will keep me from working with your children.")

Some other adults said, "We have to be out of town too often on weekends." (But the porno book dealer said, "We're willing to stay in town weekends to sell smut to your children.") Still other adults said, "I'm unsuited, untrained, and unable to work with children or preschoolers." (But the movie producer said, "We'll study, survey, and spend millions to produce whatever turns kids on.")

Some other adults said, "I could never give the time required to plan and go to teacher meetings." (But the drug pusher, the porno book dealer, and the movie producer said, "We'll stay open whatever hours are necessary every day to win the minds of the kids.")

So the adults stayed in their classes and enjoyed the sweet fellowship, absorbed good Bible study, and went out of town often on the weekends. And when Sunday came, the children went to their classes. But no one was there except the faithful few who went from one room to another, assuring them that someone would surely come to teach them soon. But no one ever came.

201. THE QUITTER

I've taught a class for many years;
Borne many burdens, toiled through tears—
But folks don't notice me a bit,
I'm so discouraged; I'll just quit.

I've led young people day and night
And sacrificed to lead them right;
But folks won't help me out a bit—
And I'm so tired; I think I'll quit.

Christ's cause is hindered everywhere
And people are dying in despair.
The reason why? Just think a bit—
The church is full of those who quit.

—Author unknown

20
Thanksgiving Messages

202. THANKSGIVING AND PRAISE

Lord, we thank thee for the beauty
Of the land in which we live;
Thank thee for the friends and loved ones
Thou so graciously doth give.

Lord, we thank thee for the blessings
That thy presence doth impart,
Peace that passeth understanding,
Joy that satisfies the heart.

Lord, we praise thee for the Giver
Who has claimed us as His own;
Who, though Lord of highest heaven,
Makes our humble hearts His home.

—Neva Brien

203. COUNT THEM ONE BY ONE

Perhaps we have not counted
All our blessings one by one;

Perhaps we have not bothered
  To remember whence they come;
And maybe we have taken
  Just for granted all the things
That the good Lord has created
  And the gifts that nature brings.

The autumn hills in glory robed,
  A golden field of grain,
A sunset's dazzling splendor
  Or the Milky Way's great plain,
The starry sky's sublimity,
  The ocean's mighty power,
The wonder of creation
  In the petal of a flower.

And so if we have failed to show
  By work or act or deed
That we are thankful unto him
  Who fills our daily need,
May this day show we're grateful
  When we add up all the sum
Of the blessings we remember,
  As we count them one by one.

—Author unknown

204. WE GIVE THANKS

Dear Lord, we give thee thanks today
  For all the blessings that we know,
Kneeling with grateful hearts, the way
  The pilgrims knelt so long ago.

For happy homes with hearthfire's glow,
  Dear Lord, we give thee thanks today,
For summer's rain and winter's snow,
  For joyful hours of work and play.

We take so little time to pray,
  Forgive us that we careless grow.
Dear Lord, we give thee thanks today,
  "Praise God from whom all blessings flow."

Whate'er the future may bestow,
  Give us, dear Lord, the strength to say
Through cloud or sunshine, weal or woe,
  Dear Lord, we give thee thanks today.

—White Heather

205. THANK YOU, LORD

Just this once, Lord, I want to come to you without problems simply to say Thank you:

For your forgiveness when I fail.

For the sheer joy of sleep when I'm terribly tired.

For the silent strength of humility when pride overtakes me.

For the justice of your laws when men are cruel.

For the remedies for sickness when I am ill.

For the simplicity of orderliness when I face confusion.

For the assurance that you have made a place especially for me when I feel inadequate among my peers.

For the joy of helping others when I see people in need,

For the earthly evidences of your will when I'm trying to find out what life is all about.

For the reality of your world when I stray too far into fantasy.

For the rightness of reasonableness when I panic too quickly.

For the fun that refreshes when everything gets too serious.

For the renewal in moments of silence when I'm dizzy from being busy in a hectic world.

Thank you, Lord, for all these things. But most of all, thank you for your abiding presence that makes every day I live a day of thanks.

206. THANKFULNESS

Thankfulness is being glad
  For good things every day;
It's showing joy by sharing
  In a kindly, thoughtful way.

It is remembering God gives
  And cares for every need;
Thankfulness is loving God
  In heart and word and deed.

—Author unknown

207. THE ART OF THANKSGIVING

The art of thanksgiving is thanksliving. It is gratitude in action. It is applying Albert Schweitzer's philosophy: "In gratitude for your own good fortune you must render in return some sacrifice of your life for other life."

Thanksgiving is thanking God for the gift of life by living it triumphantly.

It is thanking God for your talents and abilities by accepting them as obligations to be invested for the common good.

It is thanking God for all that men and women have done for you by doing things for others.

It is thanking God for opportunities by accepting them as a challenge to achievement.

It is thanking God for happiness by striving to make others happy.

It is thanking God for beauty by helping to make the world more beautiful.

It is thanking God for inspiration by trying to be an inspiration to others.

It is thanking God for health and strength by the care and reverence you show your body.

It is thanking God for the creative ideas that enrich life by adding your own creative contributions to human progress.

It is thanking God for each new day by living it to the fullest.

It is thanking God by giving hands, arms, legs, and voice to your thankful spirit.

It is adding to your prayers of thanksgiving, acts of thanksliving.

—*Wilferd A. Peterson*

208. IN EVERYTHING GIVE THANKS

For all that God in mercy sends—
For health and children, home and friends;
For comfort in the time of need,
For every kindly word or deed,
For happy thoughts and holy talk,
For guidance in our daily walk—
In everything give thanks.

—Author unknown

21
Youth and Their Needs

---

209. THE ENTHUSIASM OF YOUTH

Alfred Tennyson wrote his first book at age eighteen.

Columbus was twenty-eight when he announced his plans to find India.

Napoleon had conquered Italy at twenty-five.

John Smith staked out a colonial empire in Virginia at twenty-seven.

Newton made some of his greatest discoveries before he was twenty-five.

Joan of Arc was a heroine at nineteen.

Patrick Henry cried, "Give me liberty or give me death" at twenty-seven.

Jesus was thirty when He preached the Sermon on the Mount.

God give us more youth who are fired with the enthusiasm of high ideals!

210. HINTS FOR STUDENTS TAKING FINAL EXAMS

1. Remember that "this shall pass" (even though you may not).

2. Do your best. Study your hardest. Commit the results to God.

3. Do not expect God to rescue you from your own lack of discipline.

4. There is a point of diminishing returns in your studying. Do not allow yourself to become physically, emotionally, and spiritually drained. Being well-rested will make you more effective for the exam.

5. Do not study just to make a good grade on the test. Instead, focus on learning important material as completely as possible.

6. Place "the final" final first on your priority list: "Seek ye first the kingdom of God and His righteousness and all these things shall be added unto you." Don't let daily concerns crowd out eternal values.

211. WHAT TEENAGERS REALLY WANT

1. **Love.** We want parents who love us regardless of what we do. We want our fathers home in time for supper with the patience and time to discuss what happened that day.

2. **Understanding.** We want parents who will at least listen to our problems and try to understand the temptations and decisions we face.

3. **Trust.** We want parents who have confidence in us. This means, for example, telling us how to act on a date and then trusting us to do what they say.

4. **Joint Planning.** We don't want parents to dictate to us, but we do welcome their efforts to plan with us.

5. **Religion.** We want parents with strong spiritual convictions. We want them to attend church regularly, to say grace at meals, and to show other evidence of personal faith.

6. **Privacy.** We want a room to which we can retreat. Here we want to be able to store our own treasures and to pursue our hobbies.

7. **Respect.** We want parents who will treat us as individuals. We want to be accepted for our own age and not treated like children.

8. **Responsibility.** We want to share in the work and decisions of the family. We want to feel needed.

—Abigail Van Buren

212. THE HIGH SCHOOL GRADUATES' PRAYER

So many roads where I may go,
  Far more than two or three;
There's one thing now I'd like to know—
  Which is the road for me?

I must move on; I cannot stay;
  I pause on bended knee—
Help me, dear Lord, so I can know
  This is the road for me.

—Author unknown

213. TO OUR GRADUATES—FROM THEIR PARENTS

I cannot buy you a set of morals; I cannot build you a sense of responsibility; I cannot manufacture concern and compassion; I cannot make you a compelling, faithful spirit; I cannot give you ability to love.

I have no fortune to will you with which to gain popularity, make you a philanthropist, or help you leave memorials for charity.

I own no secret formula for success. I've never written a book of wisdom. I cannot send you away into the world on your own, with only beautiful pictures in your memory, for you have seen me cry faithless tears of despair; you have seen me shake my fist in anger; you have witnessed ugliness in times of weakness.

But these things which I cannot give you are all yours in Jesus Christ.

As you accept your diploma, severing your relations with high school, you step into new relationships with parents, friends, and the world. The "apronstrings" that have been lengthened as you grew up must now be cut. You have earned more than freedom from high school. You have proved yourself trustworthy, dependable, and mature enough to try your own wings, but we will be "on call" throughout your life.

You are fully accountable to God, your heavenly Father, who loves you far more than we can; who has riches in store beyond your comprehension, but who expects much more of someone as talented and capable as you.

I commit you to His care as the fire of the world tests the gold of your character—and I will be in prayer as you face the challenge of tomorrow.

214. A YOUTH'S PRAYER

To build a life that's clean, upright, secure;
God's temple that will through the year endure;
To walk courageously, stedfast, and sure—
  This is my prayer.

To dedicate my life, my youth, my all
To Christ, and then in answer to His call,
To be faithful to each task—the large, the small—
  This is my prayer.

—Author unknown

22
Miscellaneous

---

215. THE SNAKE THAT POISONS EVERYTHING

It topples governments, wrecks marriages, ruins careers, and destroys reputations; causes heartaches, nightmares, and indigestion; spawns suspicion, generates grief, and dispatches innocent people to sob and cry on their pillows. Even the name of this snake hisses. It is called gossip—office gossip, party gossip, neighborhood gossip, even church gossip.

Before you repeat a story, ask yourself, Is it true? Is it fair? Is it necessary? If not, then let the story die with you.

216. WHAT IS GOD LIKE?

1. God is eternal. God has always lived. He will always live. All people who live on the earth will grow old and die. But God can never grow old or die (Heb. 1:10–12).

2. God is all-powerful. Human beings are weak and limited. But God can do anything. We can trust the promises of God because He has the power to fulfill them.

3. God is all-knowing. It is possible to hide things from the eyes of people, but nothing can be hidden from God (Prov. 5:21; 1 John 3:20).

4. God is unchanging. Everything in the world changes. Even our bodies change as we grow older. But God never changes. He is the same yesterday, today, and forever (Mal. 3:6).

5. God is holy and righteous. Unlike man, God is free of sin. He is holy and righteous in His character. To worship God is to seek this same holiness and righteousness in our own lives (Ps. 11:7).

6. God is merciful. God loves us. Although He hates sin, He will forgive our sins if we truly repent (Ps. 103:8).

217. IN REMEMBRANCE

In remembrance, Lord, I come
Before thy table spread,
Of thy body pierced for me,
Thy blood so freely shed.

Though unworthy, Lord, am I,
Grant me thy pardoning grace;
Take away the sin that hides
From me thy glorious face.

—Author unknown

218. CHARACTERISTICS OF A DEACON

The following characteristics of a deacon are spelled out in Acts 6:1–8 and 1 Timothy 3:8–13:

1. A deacon is a servant, not a church boss. The word "deacon" means *servant*. A deacon is elected not to honor a person but to honor and serve God and His church.

2. A deacon is one whose character is exemplary. His life as well as his reputation is a credit to the church and the Savior. His family life sets a good example.

3. A deacon is spiritually-minded, "full of the Holy Spirit," as the Bible says. The deacon should be free of worldly entanglements.

4. A deacon is a faithful steward, "not greedy of filthy lucre." He must lead by example if the church is to grow a membership of tithers.

5. A deacon is regular in attendance at all services. By his presence he adds much; by his absence he causes much harm.

6. A deacon is a soul-winner. His earnest desire is to see people saved.

7. A deacon is the pastor's friend. He should be counselor, confidant, comforter, and companion to the minister.

219. HOW TO MAKE A FAILURE OUT OF LIFE

1. Follow the line of least resistance. Be neutral on moral and spiritual issues. Straddle the fence.

2. Alienate yourself from the church membership. Go to church when you feel like it and when it is most convenient.

3. Indulge your carnal appetites. Take it easy on Sunday and never go to church. Be lazy and selfish. Accept the pleasures offered by the world.

4. Look at the inconsistencies and sins of others. Pick flaws, find faults, and criticize. Ignore your own faults.

5. Unite with worldly organizations. Become a member of some club or fraternity. They do lots of good, and you don't have to compromise your convictions to belong.

6. Run around with people who have nothing to do with Christ and His church. Don't bring religion into your social life.

7. Eclipse your salvation with worldly interests. After all, you have a living to make. Put dollars and business ahead of your commitment to Christ.

220. SEVEN STEPS TOWARD SAVING THE SUMMER FOR THE SAVIOR

1. **Faithful attendance:** "Not forsaking the assembling of ourselves together" (Heb. 10:25).

2. **Active participation:** "Grow up into Him in all things, which is the head, even Christ" (Eph. 4:15–16).

3. **Greater effort:** "Whatsoever thy hand findeth to do, do it with thy might" (Eccles. 9:10).

4. **Intensified visitation:** "Go out into the highways and hedges, and compel them to come in" (Luke 14:23).

5. **Renewed concern:** "Lift up your eyes, and look on the fields; for they are white already to harvest" (John 4:35).

6. **Regular giving:** "Upon the first day of the week let every one of you lay by him in store, as God hath prospered" (1 Cor. 16:2).

7. **Continued growth:** "But grow in grace, and in the knowledge of our Lord and Saviour Jesus Christ" (2 Peter 3:18).

Record
of Publication

Item No.	Where Published	When Published
————	————————————	————
————	————————————	————
————	————————————	————
————	————————————	————
————	————————————	————
————	————————————	————
————	————————————	————
————	————————————	————
————	————————————	————
————	————————————	————
————	————————————	————

Item No.	Where Published	When Published
————	————————————	————
————	————————————	————
————	————————————	————
————	————————————	————
————	————————————	————
————	————————————	————
————	————————————	————
————	————————————	————
————	————————————	————
————	————————————	————
————	————————————	————
————	————————————	————
————	————————————	————
————	————————————	————
————	————————————	————
————	————————————	————
————	————————————	————
————	————————————	————
————	————————————	————
————	————————————	————
————	————————————	————

Item No.	Where Published	When Published
————	————————————	————
————	————————————	————
————	————————————	————
————	————————————	————
————	————————————	————
————	————————————	————
————	————————————	————
————	————————————	————
————	————————————	————
————	————————————	————
————	————————————	————
————	————————————	————
————	————————————	————
————	————————————	————
————	————————————	————
————	————————————	————
————	————————————	————
————	————————————	————
————	————————————	————
————	————————————	————

Item No.	Where Published	When Published
_____	_____	_____
_____	_____	_____
_____	_____	_____
_____	_____	_____
_____	_____	_____
_____	_____	_____
_____	_____	_____
_____	_____	_____
_____	_____	_____
_____	_____	_____
_____	_____	_____
_____	_____	_____
_____	_____	_____
_____	_____	_____
_____	_____	_____
_____	_____	_____
_____	_____	_____
_____	_____	_____
_____	_____	_____
_____	_____	_____
_____	_____	_____
_____	_____	_____

Item No.	Where Published	When Published

Item No.	Where Published	When Published
————	————————————	————
————	————————————	————
————	————————————	————
————	————————————	————
————	————————————	————
————	————————————	————
————	————————————	————
————	————————————	————
————	————————————	————
————	————————————	————
————	————————————	————
————	————————————	————
————	————————————	————
————	————————————	————
————	————————————	————
————	————————————	————
————	————————————	————
————	————————————	————
————	————————————	————
————	————————————	————

Item No.	Where Published	When Published
————	—————————	————
————	—————————	————
————	—————————	————
————	—————————	————
————	—————————	————
————	—————————	————
————	—————————	————
————	—————————	————
————	—————————	————
————	—————————	————
————	—————————	————
————	—————————	————
————	—————————	————
————	—————————	————
————	—————————	————
————	—————————	————
————	—————————	————
————	—————————	————
————	—————————	————
————	—————————	————
————	—————————	————

Item No.	Where Published	When Published
————	————————————————	———————
————	————————————————	———————
————	————————————————	———————
————	————————————————	———————
————	————————————————	———————
————	————————————————	———————
————	————————————————	———————
————	————————————————	———————
————	————————————————	———————
————	————————————————	———————
————	————————————————	———————
————	————————————————	———————
————	————————————————	———————
————	————————————————	———————
————	————————————————	———————
————	————————————————	———————
————	————————————————	———————
————	————————————————	———————
————	————————————————	———————
————	————————————————	———————

Item No.	Where Published	When Published
———	————————————	———————
———	————————————	———————
———	————————————	———————
———	————————————	———————
———	————————————	———————
———	————————————	———————
———	————————————	———————
———	————————————	———————
———	————————————	———————
———	————————————	———————
———	————————————	———————
———	————————————	———————
———	————————————	———————
———	————————————	———————
———	————————————	———————
———	————————————	———————
———	————————————	———————
———	————————————	———————
———	————————————	———————
———	————————————	———————

Item No.	Where Published	When Published
_____	_____	_____
_____	_____	_____
_____	_____	_____
_____	_____	_____
_____	_____	_____
_____	_____	_____
_____	_____	_____
_____	_____	_____
_____	_____	_____
_____	_____	_____
_____	_____	_____
_____	_____	_____
_____	_____	_____
_____	_____	_____
_____	_____	_____
_____	_____	_____
_____	_____	_____
_____	_____	_____
_____	_____	_____
_____	_____	_____